HOMEOPATHY A-Z

Dana Ullman, M.P.H.

Hay House, Inc.
Carlsbad, California • Sydney, Australia
Canada • Hong Kong • United Kingdom

Published and distributed in the United States by:
Hay House, Inc., P.O. Box 5100, Carlsbad, CA 92018-5100 ▪ (800) 654-5126 ▪ (800) 650-5115 (fax)

Edited by: Jill Kramer   *Designed by:* Jenny Richards

Library of Congress Cataloging-in-Publication Data

Ullman, Dana
    Homeopathy A-Z / Dana Ullman.
        p.   cm
    Includes bibliographical references.
    ISBN 1-56170-573-X (hardcover) ▪ ISBN 1-56170-798-8 (tradepaper)
    1. Homeopathy—Popular works.   I. Title.
RX76.U467   1999
615.5'32—dc21   98-29140
                                                                                   CIP

ISBN 1-56170-798-8

05 04 03 02   6 5 4 3
1st printing, January 1999
3rd printing, August 2002

Printed in China by Palace Press

CONTENTS

PART I:
ABOUT HOMEOPATHY

Homeopathy:
Medicine for the 21st Century

Homeopathy has been aptly characterized as a "medicine for the 21st century." It is a powerful yet gentle method of augmenting a person's own immune and defense system. It is a sophisticated method of individualizing medicines to the totality of physical and psychological aspects of an individual, not simply to his or her disease; and it is a tried-and-true method of healing people who experience a wide range of acute, chronic, and even hereditary ailments.

That said, it must also be acknowledged that homeopathy is not a cure-all. Homeopathy cannot cure everything or everyone. Some people's immune and defense systems are so weakened or compromised that nothing can elicit a healing response. Some people require surgery for healing to occur, and some cannot be healed for unknown reasons.

Despite these limitations for select individuals, homeopathy can often profoundly improve a person's health. It can not only provide relief for an ailment; it can precipitate a true cure. Homeopathy can help heal various physical complaints and can transform and improve a person's emotional and mental state. It can also help heal various diseases and prevent new ones from developing.

Although these statements are indeed bold, homeopathy has over 200 years of evidence to support these claims. The primary reason that homeopathy became popular in the 19th century was due to the remarkable results that homeopathic physicians experienced in treating people suffering from the infectious-disease epidemics that raged at the time. Epidemics of cholera, scarlet fever, typhoid, and yellow fever were rampant and killed large numbers of people. Yet, death rates in homeopathic hospitals were commonly one-half or even one-eighth of the death rates in conventional medical hospitals.

These magnificent results helped homeopathy grow in the United States, so much so that by the turn of the 20th century, there were 22 homeopathic medical schools, including Boston University, University of Michigan, New York (Homeopathic) Medical College, and the University of Minnesota, among others. Approximately 15 percent of American doctors considered themselves homeopathic physicians, and there were over 100 homeopathic hospitals.

Homeopathy's popularity declined sharply after the turn of the century, primarily due to the active efforts of the American Medical Association and its collaboration with American drug companies.

But although homeopathy's status in the U.S. declined, homeopathy in Europe and parts of Asia continued to grow. Between 30 and 40 percent of French doctors and 20 percent of German doctors prescribe homeopathic medicines. Over 40 percent of British doctors refer patients to homeopathic doctors, and 45 percent of Dutch physicians consider these natural medicines to be effective. Homeopathy is so popular in Europe today that it is no longer appropriate to consider it "alternative medicine" there.

Homeopathy is even more popular in parts of Asia. There are over 125 four- and five-year homeopathic colleges in India, and there are over 100,000 homeopathic doctors. Homeopathy is used in virtually every country in the world today, and millions of people take a homeopathic medicine on a daily basis.

With this background, one must now ask the question . . .

What Is Homeopathy, Anyway?

Primary Assumption: Respecting the Wisdom of the Human Body

The basic assumption behind homeopathy is that symptoms of illness are not simply something "wrong" with the person but are actually responses and efforts of the organism to defend and heal itself against infection and/or stress. The human organism does not become ill by surrendering to these forces, but as a result of the body's efforts to fight them.

Every organism survives because it has incredible adaptive capabilities, and one of the ways that an organism adapts is through the creation of symptoms. The inflammatory process is one of the important ways that an organism begins to learn what has infected it and how to deal with it. So, the creation of symptoms is one of the ways that the organism learns to live in its environment.

On the one hand, conventional medical thinking maintains great respect for the human organism, its defensive functions, and its symptoms; yet on the other hand, it commonly assumes that symptoms must be inhibited, suppressed, and controlled. Fevers must be lowered, inflammation must be suppressed, and discharges must be stopped.

Because these symptoms are important ways in which the human organism is trying to heal itself, efforts that impede this process tend to provide short-term relief for pain and discomfort, but also tend to create more long-term health problems. For instance, basic pathology texts affirm that fever is an important effort that the body deploys to fight and burn out infection, that inflammation is vital for the body to wall off pathogenic material, and that discharge is an essential way that the organism expels dead cells and infective organisms. Therapies or drugs that suppress the body's natural defenses create new, deeper, and more chronic health problems.

Inherent in conventional medical thinking about health is the assumption that whatever the body is doing is "wrong." Conversely, inherent in homeopathic thinking is the assumption that there is an internal wisdom to the human organism. This difference in assumptions leads to completely different approaches to healing.

It is useful to note that the very word *symptom* is derived from Greek and means "sign" or "signal." A symptom is best understood not as the disease itself, but as a sign or signal of the disease. Treating the sign or signal is akin to unscrewing a flashing oil light on a car. Although this treatment "works" (the light goes off!), it does not solve the fundamental problem.

Remember: The symptom is a signal of something; don't simply unplug the signal!

The Principle of Similars

If one recognizes that symptoms are beneficial responses of the organism to defend and heal itself, the primary principle of homeopathy, called "the principle of similars," is completely logical. The principle of similars refers to an ancient method that created profound healing by utilizing small doses of a substance individually chosen for its capacity to cause symptoms similar to those that the sick person is experiencing.

Because symptoms are actually defenses of the body, using a medicinal substance that causes and mimics these defenses augments a person's healing abilities.

It is not simply a coincidence that two of the very few conventional medical treatments that augment immune response are immunizations and allergy treatments, both of which are ultimately based on the homeopathic principle of similars and using "like to treat like."

The following example may be instructive at this point: A homeopath may give a very small and specially prepared dose of coffee (*Coffea cruda*) to a person who has a migraine headache and has difficulty falling asleep. Because coffee is known to cause such headaches, as well as insomnia, homeopathic doses of it will help to heal a person who suffers from these symptoms. The trick to making homeopathic medicines work effectively is to find the correct, individually chosen remedy that has the capacity to cause, if given in overdose, the similar symptoms that the sick person is experiencing.

Individualize the Remedy to the Person, Not Just the Disease

It is important to understand that there is no one remedy for every disease, because each person experiences his or her unique variation of a disease. For instance, people with a headache may experience many similar symptoms, but some people will have a headache in the front part of the head, and others in the back part. Some will have head pain worse in the morning, others worse in the late afternoon or evening. Still others will have head pain relieved by hot applications, others from cold applications; and some will have dizziness with the head pain, while others will have nausea, sore throat, or fever.

It is amazing how well we have been effectively but inaccurately indoctrinated into thinking that people with the same disease should receive the same medicine.

In actual fact, each person has his or her own "syndrome" of disease, and the most scientific way to treat this person is through the homeopathic method mentioned above.

The Experimental Basis of Every Homeopathic Medicine

In order to determine what condition a homeopathic medicine is effective in treating, a medicinal substance undergoes an experiment in toxicology called a "proving." A proving is a trial on healthy human subjects to determine what a substance causes in overdose. These experiments are typically conducted on healthy people because if they are done on people who are ill, it becomes difficult to separate out which symptoms a substance causes distinct from which symptoms the sick person is experiencing as a part of his or her illness.

Provings are usually conducted with extremely small, homeopathic prepared doses of a substance. The 30th potency of a medicine is commonly used, and the subjects are told to take the medicine once or twice daily until symptoms develop and then to stop and carefully observe what symptoms the substance elicits.

Not all subjects experience symptoms of a proving, and generally, those people who develop symptoms experience them for a couple of days to a couple of weeks.

People who volunteer to do a proving are asked to keep a diary and to list obvious or subtle physical or psychological symptoms that they experience. They are encouraged to describe in detail the precise type of pain or discomfort and what types of things aggravate or ameliorate them.

This careful cataloging of symptoms helps homeopaths develop texts and computer software, even expert systems, that enable them to prescribe the homeopathic remedy accurately for sick people who have similar symptoms as the substance's.

Homeopaths also utilize information about the toxicity of a substance from standard toxicology texts. However, the homeopathic provings provide a considerably more detailed description of the subtle physical and psychological symptoms that a substance creates.

The Unique Homeopathic Pharmaceutical Process

Homeopathic medicines are made from various plants, minerals, animals, or chemicals. Ultimately, every substance on the planet is a potential medicine, and that's because every substance on the planet is also potentially toxic.

The way that homeopaths reduce the potential for toxicity and actually increase the potential for healing is through a specific pharmaceutical process that is unique to homeopathy called *potentization*. Potentization refers to a process of sequential dilution with vigorous shaking in between each dilution.

More specifically, the tincture of a plant may be diluted in double distilled water (usually in a 1:10 or 1:100 dilution). This mixture is vigorously shaken and then diluted again 1:10 or 1:100. This process of dilution and shaking is repeated 3, 6, 12, 30, 200, 1,000, 10,000, 50,000, or more times.

When a substance is diluted 1:10 six times, it is called a "6X" potency. When a substance is diluted 1:100 six times, it is called a "6C" potency. The simple way to remember this is that "X" is the Roman numeral for 10, and "C" is the Roman numeral for 100.

The surprising and startling part of homeopathic medicine is that 200 years of experience by hundreds of thousands of homeopathic doctors and by tens of millions of homeopathic patients has confirmed that the more a medicine is potentized, the longer and deeper it acts, and the fewer doses are necessary to effect a curative response.

Why Homeopathy Makes Sense

Homeopathy's principle of similars makes a profound contribution to understanding healing, because inherent in this principle is a deep respect for the wisdom of the human body. Homeopathy's emphasis on individualizing a medicine to the totality of a person's symptoms, not just a person's specific disease, is also wonderfully logical.

The difficult-to-understand part of homeopathy has to do with the extreme microdoses used. In fact, according to present laws of physics, once a homeopathic medicine is diluted 1:10 24 times or 1:100 12 times, there should be no remaining molecules of the original substance.

Homeopaths acknowledge that there may not be any remaining molecules left in such medicines, but they also assert that a more powerful energy, essence, or information of the original substance seems to remain, and actually increases with each potentization. They assert that 200 years of clinical experience by homeopaths throughout the world have confirmed and continue to confirm this observation. They acknowledge that they don't know how their medicines work, though various individuals have developed compelling theories.

Recently, Shui-Yin Lo, Ph.D., a physicist from the California Institute of Technology, discovered that a nonmelting ice crystal that maintains an electrical field is created in room-temperature water when a medicinal substance is placed in a double-distilled purified water and then diluted 1:10 at least seven times and shaken in between each dilution.

Dr. Lo and his colleagues have taken photographs of these electric ice crystals, and at least a dozen leading scientists at various major universities have confirmed their biological activity.

Homeopaths have long assumed that homeopathic remedies are "energy medicines." Akin to concepts of energy, "chi," or "ki" in acupuncture, homeopathic medicines are thought to resonate with the energetic essence of the individual to elicit a healing response.

Whether or not it is ever confirmed how or why homeopathic medicines work, there is little doubt in the minds and hearts of homeopaths and their patients that these natural remedies work extraordinarily well.

While homeopaths acknowledge that they don't know how their remedies work, it must also be noted that there are a lot of conventional medical treatments today for which the precise mechanism of action remains a mystery. The bigger question is: Do homeopathic medicines work? The following section will begin to answer this important question.

Evidence That Homeopathy Works

There is actually a lot more scientific evidence that homeopathic medicines work than most people realize. There is certainly strong evidence that homeopathic medicines are more than a placebo.

Before discussing formal scientific studies, there are other types of evidence showing that homeopathic medicines are biologically active and clinically therapeutic:

1. Homeopathy gained its greatest popularity in Europe and the U.S. in the 19th century primarily because of the very impressive result shown in treating the infectious-disease epidemics that ravaged populations at that time, including cholera, scarlet fever, yellow fever, and typhoid,

among others. It is unlikely that a placebo could be as effective as homeopathic medicines were.

2. Homeopathic medicines are commonly effective in treating acute and chronic conditions in various animals, oftentimes providing dramatic results. While animals can be influenced by tenderness and love, it is unlikely that they would get the same impressive results that veterinarians and others using homeopathic medicines obtain.

3. Homeopathic medicines are commonly effective in treating infants, who are also susceptible to a placebo effect, but once again, the dramatic results that are experienced using homeo-

pathic medicines to treat teething or colicky infants or those suffering from a raging ear infection are rarely experienced with a simple placebo.

4. Approximately 20 percent of people with chronic diseases who are prescribed homeopathic medicines experience a healing crisis; that is, they temporarily experience an exacerbation of certain symptoms prior to a significant improvement in their chronic disease and their overall health. It is rare for people who are given a placebo to have experienced this frequency of initial worsening of symptoms prior to improvement.

In addition to this historical evidence, there is also a body of laboratory experiments that have shown biological activity from homeopathic medicines, and a body of clinical experiments that have shown the efficacy of homeopathic treatment.

In light of clinical studies, a team of German and American physicians and scientists published in *The Lancet* (September 20, 1997) a review of 89 clinical studies. They found that on average those patients given a homeopathic medicine were 2.45 times more likely to experience a positive result than those given a placebo. This review of research evaluated various experiments that tested the efficacy of homeopathic remedies in the treatment of hay fever, asthma, migraine headache, ear infection, upper respiratory infection, rheumatoid arthritis, diarrhea, indigestion, influenza, childbirth, postsurgical complications, varicose veins, sprains and strains, among many others.

Even a skeptic of homeopathy who responded in *The Lancet* to this research admitted that this review of research was "completely state of the art."

Despite the progress that has been made recently in verifying the efficacy of homeopathic medicine, there is still a great need for more research and for replication of these studies by independent researchers.

Differentiating Real Healing from Merely Suppressing Disease

Just because symptoms disappear shortly after any treatment does not necessarily mean that a "cure" has been effected. This experience can mean one of several things:

— The symptoms went away on their own, and the treatment had nothing to do with it.

— The treatment lessened the intensity of the symptoms, providing short-term relief but resulting in the recurrence of symptoms in the near future.

— The treatment suppressed the symptoms, pushing them deeper into the body. Although suppression may cause the initial symptoms to disappear, they are replaced with more serious, deeper symptoms that are more discomforting and potentially dangerous.

The concept of suppressing symptoms is well accepted and understood in psychology. It is commonly observed that when a person suppresses his or her emotions, it pushes the emotional turmoil deeper, leading the person to explode at some future time, often at people who are not directly related to the origin of the person's problem.

While people may be familiar with the problems associated with the suppression of emotions, people are generally not familiar with the possibility that many conventional medical treatments can suppress their physical symptoms, driving the disease deeper into the person.

Such is the problem when using pharmacological agents that are explicitly prescribed for their ability to control or inhibit symptoms that are the natural defensive functions of the body.

The father of American homeopathy was a German physician named Constantine Hering, M.D. He observed that people go through a specific healing process after being given the correct homeopathic medicine. He developed guidelines in which to determine when a real healing is taking place. These guidelines have been called "Hering's laws of cure," but some homeopaths prefer to call them Hering's guidelines of cure.

To understand these guidelines, it is first useful to know that homeopaths carefully evaluate the evolution of a person's physical, emotional, and mental/spiritual symptoms. Homeopaths consider mental/spiritual symptoms to be deepest to the core of a person's being, for they represent the will, the ego, the sense of security that the person feels, and the person's overall state of consciousness. The emotional symptoms are external to the mental/spiritual level of the person because imbalances in the deeper level will create various fears, angers, depressive states, and other emotions. The physical symptoms are the most outer manifestation of the person, though every level can and will influence the other.

Also, each level has certain symptoms that have more or less influence on a person's overall health. For instance, a person's asthma will be deeper than his or her skin rash, a person's fear of death will be deeper than his or her irritability, and a person's loss of self-esteem will be deeper than a subtle reduction in memory. Likewise, when comparing symptoms on different levels, a person's heart disease will more profoundly affect his or her health than a difficulty in concentration experienced on the mental/spiritual level.

In light of these levels of the human being and the degrees of intensity to which a symptom impairs a person's ability to live, Hering found that healing progresses:

— from within to without (from the deepest part of our being to the most external);

— from the most recent disease back in time to previous ones (a reversion of the disease process); and

— from the top of the body to the bottom of the body.

Homeopaths observe that a truly effective therapy sometimes elicits a temporary exacerbation of certain symptoms, usually in the superficial ones, or those that the person had many years previously. Homeopaths assert that a true healing is taking place when a person's current symptoms are more superficial than previous ones.

On the other hand, if and when a person's symptoms disappear and new ones that are more serious develop, this suggests that the treatment has suppressed the person's condition and has made the symptoms worse. Unknown to most physicians and patients, people undergoing conventional medical treatment are commonly having their disease suppressed. Homeopaths assert that one of the reasons that there is increased mental disease and increased chronic disease at earlier and earlier ages is because of effective suppression of the disease process by conventional medical treatment.

Distinct from methods that suppress disease are those that help disease express and externalize itself. Homeopathy's use of the principle of similars is one important safeguard against disease suppression because it mimics the wisdom of the body rather than suppresses its symptoms.

How to Make Homeopathy Work for You

The trick to making homeopathic medicines work for you is to find the individualized remedy that most closely fits the symptoms that you are experiencing. There will sometimes be more than one remedy that fits the sick person's symptoms. In such cases, consider giving the remedy that fits the person's most intense symptoms, giving priority to a remedy that matches a person's psychological state.

Readers are encouraged to obtain other homeopathic guidebooks to help them find the individualized homeopathic remedy for them, their sick family member, or their friends. Although there may be some overlapping of information from these books, each book also has some information that the others don't have that can help you help use homeopathic medicines most effectively.

One of the great benefits of homeopathy is the often dramatic results that the remedies provide when a person is experiencing much pain or discomfort. Generally, a person will notice observable changes within a couple of hours or after a single night's rest.

People with chronic symptoms or ailments will sometimes require more time before they experience noticeable results from homeopathic medicines. It should also be noted that it is highly recommended to seek out professional homeopathic care if and when a person has chronic or recurring symptoms or for any severe acute ailment. This book may provide information on remedies that may provide some relief from these symptoms, but more profound results can often be obtained from the care of a professional homeopath (see "The Place for Professional Homeopathic Care" later in this section).

This book primarily recommends that people use the 6th, 12th, or 30th potencies. Generally, when you are extremely confident in the selection of the remedy, consider giving the 30th potency. When you are not confident in the selection of the remedy, consider giving the 6th potency. When you are somewhere in between, give the 12th potency. If you have a homeopathic medicine kit at home and the potency that you need is not in the kit, simply give whatever potency you have.

Information about the number of doses to give of a remedy is provided during the discussion of each ailment, but the basic idea in homeopathy is to give as few doses of the remedy as is possible but as much as is necessary. Homeopathic medicines do not work by the notion of "the more the merrier."

Because homeopathic medicines catalyze a person's body to heal itself, it is often unnecessary to give many doses. Homeopathic medicines are like a match; they get a fire going. After the fire is burning, it isn't typically necessary to strike another match unless the flame dies down. Repeating a dose of a homeopathic medicine is necessary when a dose provides a benefit but the benefit wears off.

It is rarely necessary to take a homeopathic medicine more than a couple of days.

People should seriously consider having a homeopathic medicine kit in their home, because children, in particular, tend to get ill at night when pharmacies and health food stores are often closed. Homeopathic medicine kits can be small (six remedies) or considerably larger (28–50 remedies). These kits are available at homeopathic pharmacies and homeopathic distributors, as well as at select health food stores (see the Resources section for a listing of sources of them).

Homeopathic medicine kits are primarily "single" ingredient remedies that people must learn how to use from various homeopathic self-care books like this one. In addition to having these single ingredient remedies, it is useful to have some of the homeopathic combination remedies in the home as well. Information about these combination remedies is provided in the next section.

Classical Homeopathy and Commercial Homeopathy: The Interface

"Classical homeopathy" refers to the use of homeopathic medicines according to the original principles of homeopathy, including:

— the use of a single homeopathic medicine at a time;

— the strict individualization of a medicine to the person, not simply to the disease that they have; and

— the use of the minimum dose necessary to elicit a healing.

Early in the development of homeopathy, some practitioners and pharmacies chose to combine several homeopathic medicines together in a formula that would then be given to a wide variety of people who had the same disease. Called "combination medicines," "complexes," or "homeopathic formulas," these remedies are commonly available in health food stores and pharmacies. These products are usually marketed based on the name of the condition that they treat (that is, cold, flu, colic, teething, allergy, sinusitis, headache, arthritis, etc.), while single remedies are marketed by the specific ingredient that it is. Typically, a homeopathic manufacturer chooses two to ten of the most common remedies found to be effective in treating people suffering from a specific ailment.

Because homeopathic combination remedies do not follow the original principles of classical homeopathy, some homeopaths assert that this is not "real homeopathy."

Whatever one's attitudes about homeo-pathic combination remedies may be, it is clear that they often provide relief to people suffering from various complaints. Also, they are considerably safer than conventional drugs. While these combination remedies may not provide a deep cure of the person, the vast majority of single homeopathic medicines that are prescribed for acute ailments do not truly cure a person, but simply provide safe and effective relief.

Homeopathic combination remedies are only available for conditions that are considered nonlife-threatening. It is commonly acknowledged that a single remedy will tend to act longer and deeper than a combination remedy, but there are specific instances when a combination remedy may be appropriate:

1. When a person is suffering and he or she cannot figure out which remedy to give, a homeo-pathic combination remedy should be considered. While it is true that people can guess which remedy to give, they may be better off doing a "shotgun" approach with a combination remedy than giving a single remedy that has a smaller chance of being the correct one.

2. When you know which single remedy to give, but that remedy is not immediately available at the local health food store or pharmacy, a homeopathic combination remedy should be considered. Because many single homeopathic medicines are not always available locally, one must sometimes rely upon combination remedies.

The limitations of homeopathic combination remedies should also be acknowledged. Combination remedies should not be taken by people with serious or life-threatening problems, unless one's professional homeopath approves of such care. Combination remedies should not be prescribed for people who have chronic problems that continually return once the homeopathic medicine wears off. If and when a combination remedy doesn't work after 48 hours, it is rarely worthwhile taking for a longer period of time, though one could consider trying another company's combination remedy because it may have within it the remedy that is needed.[1]

It should also be noted that some classical homeopaths incorrectly assert that combination remedies are suppressive. There is no evidence that this is true, and further, it makes no sense. Every plant and animal product is a combination of various organic and inorganic substances, and it is therefore patently impossible that combination remedies inherently have a suppressive effect.

Readers should know that there are people who get involved in homeopathy who, like in every other field, become fundamentalists, who see their world in black and white, and who assume that there is only one way to do homeopathy (or anything else). There are many ways to make homeopathic medicines work. Indeed, there may be

certain methods that make homeopathic medicines work more effectively (and here is where classical homeopathy is so important); however, simplistic and dogmatic thinking has no place in the art and science of healing.

---

[1] Because homeopathic medicines are recognized by the U.S. Food and Drug Administration (FDA) as primarily "over-the-counter drugs" (drugs that do not require a doctor's prescription), homeopathic manufacturers are required by law to state the specific disease or ailment for which this homeopathic combination medicine is useful in treating. This is distinct from herbal remedies or supplements for which the FDA does not allow specific disease indications, but does allow manufacturers to list specific structure/function claims which the product has been proven to have.

The Place for Professional Homeopathic Care

Today, virtually every type of health professional practices homeopathic medicine, though the greatest number of homeopaths are medical doctors, naturopaths, and chiropractors. There are also numerous unlicensed homeopaths who have diligently studied homeopathy in one of the various homeopathic training programs. Although these unlicensed practitioners are not well trained in conventional diagnosis and treatment, many of them are excellent practitioners of homeopathy. Because of the inherent danger of practicing homeopathy without a medical background, people are encouraged to seek homeopathic care from someone already licensed or seek other conventional medical care concurrently.

Professional homeopathic care is usually focused on what is called "constitutional care," that is, the prescription of a homeopathic medicine that is highly individualized to a person based on his or her genetic inheritance, past health history, past medical treatment, and the totality of physical, emotional, and mental/spiritual symptoms that are presently experienced.

The concept of constitutional treatment is foreign to most people in the Western world because there is nothing like this in all of Western conventional medicine. The closest concept that Western medicine has to constitutional treatment is the idea of reducing a person's susceptibility to disease. Although Western medicine has developed specific treatments, such as immunizations, that reduce susceptibility to particular diseases, there is nothing in Western medicine that has the capacity to strengthen a person's overall resistance to disease.

The professional practice of homeopathy, like the practice of acupuncture and ayurvedic medicine, is a system of healing that is primarily based on strengthening a person's overall state of health. This strengthening helps increase resistance to various diseases and raises the person's health status.

Homeopaths are trained to find a constitutional remedy that can have profoundly positive influences on a person's health. The correct constitutional remedy can cure chronic disease, reduce the influences of hereditary diseases, strength a person's emotional and mental state, and reduce the intensity and frequency of acute ailments. Of course, this is an ideal situation. Most of the time, a constitutional medicine is not a cure-all, in that the person may still have some chronic symptoms, but they will usually be reduced in their frequency and intensity. In such instances, homeopaths observe that the constitutional remedy removes a "layer" of disease, for which another remedy is needed to help remove the next layer.

Due to the various dis-easing influences that beset a person in this lifetime and that have affected their genetic make-up, most people need to receive a series of individually chosen homeopathic medicines to effect the most profound healing.

Although one of the great benefits of professional homeopathic care is the real possibility of significant reduction, if not cure, of chronic ailments, the problem with homeopathy is that it is not always easy to find the correct medicine(s) for everyone. The results from homeopathic medicines often occur relatively fast, but it sometimes takes more than a single visit to a homeopath to find the correct remedy to start the healing process. However, because the benefits from homeopathic medicines are so great, people are encouraged to be patient with themselves and with their homeopath.

Ultimately, people can use this book to learn to treat themselves, their families, and their close friends for many common acute ailments. However, chronic and serious ailments require professional homeopathic care. Learning to know the place for self-care and the place for professional care is not always easy, but as distinct from much of conventional medicine that tends to encourage a passive patient, the patient in homeopathy plays a central, even starring role.

PART II: HOMEOPATHY A–Z

The information provided in this book about each homeopathic medicine primarily highlights the key features of a homeopathic remedy. This book was not written to provide complete information about each remedy. Readers are encouraged to complement the information provided in this book with other homeopathic guidebooks in order to learn how to use homeopathic medicines with the greatest accuracy and effectiveness.

Homeopathic medicines are listed by their Latin names because homeopaths are precise in giving reference to the specific plant, mineral, or animal species they use. A listing of the common name for each homeopathic medicine is listed on pages 147-148.

** In the A–Z list that follows, two asterisks suggest that the medicine is the most common successful remedy for the ailment in question.

A

The caduceus, the symbol of medicine, is held to one's chest, for it is the wand of the Greek god Hermes, and its two snakes represent intertwined spiritual power with winged transformational capacities.

The A-Z List

ABSCESSES

Abscesses are the skin's response to infection. Rather than attack the bacteria using antibiotic ointments or pills, homeopathic medicines augment the body's own defenses to help it heal itself.

Expect noticeable changes from the correct homeopathic medicine within 24 hours. Give the 6th, 12th, or 30th potency four times a day. It is unnecessary to give it longer than two days.

☧ Hepar sulphuris
This remedy is for abscesses that are extremely sensitive to touch, cold, or simple drafts. If cuts tend to turn into abscesses, consider this remedy.

☧ Belladonna
When an abscess is bright red and throbs, consider this medicine.

☧ Lachesis
This medicine is indicated in treating abscesses that have a bluish-purple or dark color.

☧ Silicea
When abscesses start after exposure to a foreign body (a splinter or the like), this is the first remedy to consider.

homeopathy a-z

ABUSE

Emotional support and comfort are essential in helping a person who has been physically, emotionally, or sexually abused, and homeopathic medicines can be a very important and often effective adjunct to a person's care. When people experience chronic physical or psychological symptoms after abuse, professional homeopathic care should be sought. Some type of professional psychological care, at least short-term, is generally recommended for anyone who has been abused.

Give the 30th potency of the indicated remedy every two to four hours during the first 12 hours, and then take only as needed. It is rarely necessary to take more than eight doses per episode. If strong emotions continue to return, seek professional homeopathic care.

☒ **Ignatia

This medicine is homeopathy's leading remedy for acute stages of grief. It is not only useful in relieving various emotional symptoms that an abused person feels, but also in relieving various physical symptoms that manifest in the process. This remedy is particularly indicated when people sigh frequently, have a lump in the throat, and prefer to cry when they are alone rather than in public. When they do cry, it is usually in great sobs rather than just simple tears.

☒ Staphysagria

This is a key remedy for people who have been in long-term abusive relationships. This remedy is indicated when the abused individuals have suppressed their anger until they explode. This remedy is also valuable for someone who has experienced great humiliation.

☒ Stramonium

When the person who is abused is truly terrified and if there was great violence as part of the abuse, this medicine is often extremely useful.

AIDS

Homeopathy has an impressive history of treating people with serious infectious diseases. Because homeopathy is a powerful way to strengthen a person's immune system, it is an ideal healing method for people with AIDS and people who are HIV positive. Besides being useful for a person's overall health, homeopathic medicines can be effective in treating the various acute manifestations of the disease.

Due to the seriousness of this condition, it is best to seek professional homeopathic attention for this condition.

ALLERGIES
(respiratory)

There is a body of scientific evidence to show the efficacy of homeopathic medicines in treating respiratory allergies. If you don't know which of the single remedies below are most indicated for your symptoms, consider one of the numerous homeopathic combination medicines available in health food stores and pharmacies.

The homeopathic medicines listed here will often provide noticeable results within one to three hours. If you wish to reduce the frequency and intensity of your chronically recurring allergy symptoms and if you want a treatment that may actually provide a cure for your allergies, seek professional homeopathic care.

Give the 6th, 12th, or 30th potency every two hours during intense symptoms, and every four hours during mild symptoms. It is unnecessary to take them longer than two days.

(Allergies, cont'd.)

☒ Allium cepa

If much tearing from the eyes and a thin, watery discharge that literally pours out of your nose is experienced, consider this remedy. This discharge may have a burning effect that irritates the nostrils. Symptoms are generally worse in a warm room and are relieved in a cool room or in the open air.

☒ Euphrasia

When the tears from the eyes have a burning effect that irritate and redden the cheeks, this is usually the remedy.

☒ Ambrosia

This remedy is useful for people with allergies to ragweed.

☒ Sabadilla

This medicine is effective in treating allergies with frequent, spasmodic sneezing.

☒ Solidago

People who are allergic to goldenrod benefit from this remedy.

☒ House dust mite

This is the remedy to consider for people with allergies to the house dust mite, which is the most common allergen in the world today.

homeopathy a-z

ALLERGIES (food)

Food allergies generally represent symptoms of a person's constitutional disposition and are most effectively treated by a professional homeopath. To obtain temporary relief of your symptoms, look under the specific acute symptoms you are experiencing (Indigestion, Headache, etc.).

ANGER

A book like this cannot adequately describe all of the various kinds of anger and the specific homeopathic medicines that match them. The following remedies represent a small number of the most common medicines that have anger as a primary aspect of their dis-ease.

The 12th or 30th potency is recommended, and one to six doses per episode are all that are generally needed to elicit a beneficial response. If you repeatedly feel the need to take one of the remedies below, it is best to seek professional homeopathic attention to deal with the underlying disease from which the chronic state of anger is manifesting.

☒ Nux vomica
People who benefit from this medicine are impatient types who are hard-driving, competitive, irritable, and indignant individuals who are "stressed out" and who (consciously or not) make others equally stressed out. This remedy is more com-

monly indicated in men than women. This is a common remedy for people who over-indulge in alcohol, drugs, coffee, and rich foods.

Staphysagria

A person who needs this remedy tends to suppress their anger and then express it in a rage. This person could be an abuser or the person who is abused.

Chamomilla

When a person becomes hyper-irritable, is hypersensitive to pain, and makes many demands but then rejects what is offered, consider this remedy. This medicine is most commonly indicated during infancy, during drug withdrawal, and during the end stages of life.

Sepia

This remedy is a common medicine for women going through menopause and for independent women who are assertive, aggressive, critical, and strongly insist on doing things their way. Their anger is rarely violent, but instead, a nagging, bossy irritability.

34

homeopathy a-z

ARTHRITIS

Homeopaths do not simply treat arthritis, but the *person* with arthritis. Because arthritis is usually only a part (sometimes a significant part) of the dis-ease, the homeopathic approach makes sense and is often very effective. The best results tend to occur in people who are in early onset or in people who have not taken massive doses of corticosteroidal drugs, though at least some relief can be provided to people in varying stages of arthritis with the correct remedy. The following short list is primarily to provide relief for the acute phase of the arthritic inflammation. It is best to obtain professional homeopathic care to obtain deeper and more significant relief and cure.

It is generally best to take the 6th, 12th, or 30th potency four to six times a day. Continue to take it only as long as it provides relief.

☒ **Rhus toxicodendron

This is the most common remedy for acute arthritic pain. It is indicated when people experience a "rusty-gate" syndrome of arthritis—that is, when individuals experience great pains upon initial motion, reduced pain the more they move around, and then become stiff again after resting for a while. People who benefit from this remedy also tend to be very sensitive to cold, wet weather and have aggravations of their symptoms at night and in bed.

☒ Bryonia

This remedy is indicated when arthritic pain is aggravated from any type of motion, and the more motion one does, the worse pain the person experiences. Such people tend to be irritable, constipated, and want to be alone.

☒ Apis

When a person experiences great swelling in the joint(s) with hot, burning, stinging pain, this remedy is wonderfully effective. Warm or hot applications tend to aggravate their condition, while cool and cold applications provide some relief.

☒ Belladonna

When rapid and violent onset of throbbing arthritic pain arises in red, hot, swollen joints, this is the remedy to consider.

ASTHMA

Asthma is best treated by a professional homeopath, but in the absence of such care, people can provide self-treatment for the acute phase of an asthma attack. The stronger the symptoms are, the faster the remedy usually works. Scientific research has verified that homeopathic medicines can effectively treat this and other allergic conditions.

It is recommended to use the 12th or 30th potencies. Prescribe them every hour for up to three doses, and then repeat whenever the symptoms get worse. Stay in touch with your doctor because asthma can be dangerous.

House dust mite
If you are allergic to it, a homeopathic dose of it is often effective. More people are allergic to house dust mite than any other substance, making this an important remedy for an acute attack of asthma.

Arsenicum
When fear (of suffocation, disease, and/or death), restlessness, and weakness are prominent in an asthma attack, especially when the attack occurs between midnight and 3 A.M., consider this remedy. Also, if the person is very thirsty but only drinks in sips, this suggests that *Arsenicum* may be indicated.

Spongia
When a person has dry, wheezing, labored breathing that sounds like whistling or sawing, consider this remedy. It is also indicated when the asthma attack begins after exposure to being chilled or when a dry, barking, or croupy cough is concurrent.

Ipecacuahna
Consider this remedy when a person has asthma with rattling mucus in the chest and when nausea or vomiting is concurrent with wheezing.

ATTENTION DEFICIT DISORDER (ADD)

ADD and its various syndromes is not simply a condition of children, but of all age groups. There are obviously various and differing symptoms and syndromes from which people with ADD suffer, and homeopathic medicines are uniquely well suited to their treatment because each homeopathic medicine is effective in treating a specific syndrome of physical and psychological symptoms.

However, because ADD represents a chronic condition that requires a highly individualized remedy, it is best treated by a professional homeopath.

The following remedies are not described to encourage self-treatment, but to help people realize the various syndromes in which ADD manifests and of homeopathy's individualization of treatment.

Stramonium

People who need *Stramonium* are known to experience extreme fears and exhibit violent behaviors. They are especially fearful of the dark, animals, and water. They are easily startled and will automatically, even unconsciously, respond with rage beyond proportion to the initiating event, almost as though it was an animalistic, primordial response. These tantrums may include stammering, cursing, and hitting. Most of the time, people develop the need for *Stramonium* from unknown events, although homeopaths have also found that certain birth traumas, violent abuse (physical or sexual), or traumatic events may lead to the symptoms that *Stramonium* can effectively cure.

Cina

People who need *Cina* are extremely irritable and physically aggressive. They are prone to fighting and arguing and tend to have tantrums when they are disciplined or simply told to do something. They are disposed to biting, kicking, pinching, and screaming. They benefit from being rocked, but don't like being touched, carried (except over the shoulder), or even looked at. *Cina* is a leading homeopathic medicine for pinworms. If a child has pinworms and ADD, *Cina* should be seriously considered.

Hyoscyamus

This remedy is typically indicated when people exhibit sexualized symptoms of any type or when they have manic symptoms of various sorts, such as pressured speech, great loquacity, extreme silliness, or very high energy. These people tend to be quarrelsome and obscene. They will curse, expose themselves, play with themselves, or less often, act in a seductive fashion. They are also known to be very jealous, especially when a younger sibling is born. This jealousy may even lead to malicious violence against this younger sibling. Bedwetting may be an additional concurrent complaint.

Tarentula hispanica

This remedy is useful when children or adults exhibit endless physical activity. These people are always active, always in motion. They are hurried and impatient, but they are soothed and hypnotized by music, and they love to dance. They tend to have a good sense of rhythm and like to play various instruments. However, these people have a tendency to be destructive with respect to anything they get their hands on. They even have a tendency to rip and destroy their own clothes. They need to be watched very carefully, although they can get irritated if they know they are being watched.

♨ Veratrum album

This remedy is good for restless people who have difficulty maintaining concentration, following directions, or staying at their desk. These people are constantly busy and hurried and have the unusual desire to touch and/or kiss anything. These people tend to engage in repetitive behaviors, such as stacking blocks or cutting or tearing things. They are "know-it-alls" and can be bossy, self-righteous, and argumentative.

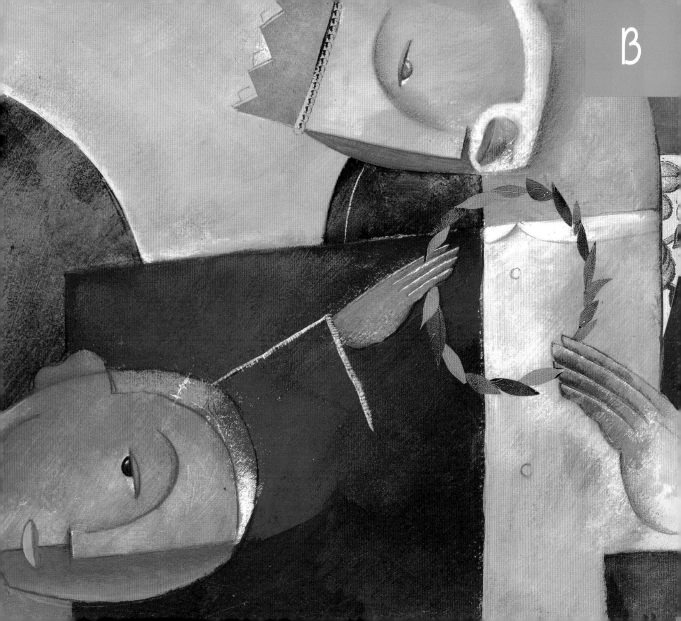

ß

A crown of herbs is bestowed upon a healer.

BACK PAIN

Homeopathic remedies have a useful place in the treatment of back pain, although massage, chiropractic, or some sort of physical therapy may also be necessary.

Use the 6th, 12th, or 30th potency every two hours in extreme pain, and approximately four times a day with mild pain. Continue to take it only as long as it provides relief. It is generally not necessary to take it more than three days straight.

☒ **Rhus toxicodendron

When pain is primarily aggravated upon initial motion and relieved by continual motion, consider this remedy. People who benefit from it tend to feel stiff if they sit or lay down for a prolonged period. Their back pain is worse at night and causes them to be very restless in bed. Sleep tends to be very fitful due to the stiffness and pain they experience.

☒ Hypericum

When back pain includes shooting pains that are the result of an injury, this remedy is indicated.

☒ Bryonia

Back pain and stiffness that is aggravated by any type of motion (even deep breathing) suggests this medicine. The pain makes people very irritable, with a strong desire to be alone.

☒ Colocynthis

Cramping or spasmodic pain that is alleviated by heat, firm pressure, or doubling up will be helped by this remedy. People who need this remedy tend to be very irritable.

homeopathy a - z

BITES AND STINGS

The following homeopathic remedies are often very effective in reducing the pain and discomfort from insect or animal bites and stings. Whether medical attention is required or not, homeopathic remedies can be used concurrently.

In addition to the remedies listed below, there are some homeopathic external gels/ointments for people who have been stung. Reapply this remedy after every washing.

Use the 6th, 12th, or 30th potency every one to two hours if the pain is intense, and reduce the frequency of the dose as the pain subsides. It is rarely necessary to take a remedy longer than 36 hours.

☒ **Ledum
Insect bites and bee stings are most commonly treated with this remedy. It is particularly good for bites or stings that are relieved by cold or ice application.

☒ Apls
When there is much swelling; and a burning, stinging pain that is aggravated by heat or warmth, consider this remedy.

☒ Staphysagrla
If a person is hypersensitive to insect bites (especially from mosquitoes), and if the bites become large and irritating, use this remedy.

BLADDER INFECTIONS

It is common for women to get a bladder infection, take an antibiotic, and then get another bladder infection. Homeopathic medicines tend to strengthen a woman's body so that repeated bladder infections are less common.

Homeopathic medicines tend to act very rapidly in providing relief from a bladder infection. Usually, the woman notices improvement within an hour, or at least after a single night's sleep. Use the 6th, 12th, or 30th potency every two hours during intense pains and every four hours in milder pain. It is rarely necessary to take it for more than two or three days.

☒ Sarsaparilla

This is the most common remedy for bladder infections. People who benefit from it tend to have severe pain at the end of urination. Less typical but confirmatory that this is the correct remedy is that the woman may have such difficulty urinating while sitting that she prefers to urinate while standing up.

☒ Cantharis

This is another common remedy for bladder infections, especially when there is a rapid onset of symptoms; a constant desire to urinate with an ability to eliminate only drops at a time; and severe pain before, during, and after urination.

☒ Staphysagria

This medicine is indicated when a person gets a bladder infection after an experience of physical or emotional abuse or from any type of embarrassment. It is also indicated for women who get a bladder infection after intercourse.

♟ Apis

Consider this medicine when there is much burning, stinging pain that is aggravated by warmth and relieved by cold, and when there is swelling of parts in the body.

♟ Sepia

When there is a strong and frequent urge to urinate but when the woman is only able to urinate a little and feels that her internal urinary organs feel extremely lax, think of this remedy. The woman may accidentally expel some urine after sneezing, coughing, or laughing.

BLEEDING

Depending on the amount and the place from which one is bleeding, medical care may be necessary. In the meantime, the following remedies can be helpful. People who have a tendency to bleed easily and profusely would benefit from professional homeopathic care.

Use the 6th, 12th, or 30th potency every hour in severe cases, and then reduce the frequency of the dose as the bleeding subsides. It is usually not necessary to take these remedies longer than 24 hours.

♟ **Arnica

This is the premier treatment for bleeding from an injury.

♟ Calendula

An external application of this remedy in a gel, ointment, or spray is usually effective in stopping bleeding from a wound.

♟ Phosphorus

Use this remedy when a person has a tendency to get frequent nosebleeds or when small wounds bleed a lot.

♟ Cinchona

Consider this remedy if a person has lost a lot of blood and/or bodily fluids and is now weak and exhausted. It is useful in helping the individual regain strength.

BLISTERS

This is a simple complaint that homeopathic remedies can easily help heal.

☒ Calendula
An external application of this remedy in a gel, ointment, or spray is usually effective in reducing the pain and swelling of a blister.

BOILS

A little boil may be a minor condition, but it can be quite painful. Luckily, homeopathic medicines can often act rapidly to heal them.

Give the 6th, 12th, or 30th potency every four hours. It is never necessary to take a remedy longer than a day.

☒ Hepar sulphuris
This remedy is for boils that are extremely sensitive to touch, cold, or simple draft. It is also useful if a cut turns into a boil.

☒ Belladonna
When a boil is bright red and throbbing, consider this remedy.

☒ Silicea
When boils start after exposure to a foreign body (a splinter or the like), this is the first remedy to consider.

BREAKUP OF A RELATIONSHIP

A good cry, support from a friend or family member, and sometimes therapy are useful in dealing with a breakup of a relationship, but homeopathic medicines are invaluable adjuncts. These natural remedies will not only help you feel better faster, but they often prevent emotional traumas of a breakup from manifesting in physical ailments.

Generally, just a couple of doses of the 30th potency of the correct remedy are needed.

☒ **Ignatia

This is the leading homeopathic remedy for people suffering from the acute grief of a broken relationship. Consider *Ignatia* when a person sighs frequently, has a lump in the throat, and tends to cry in a sobbing manner.

☒ Natrum muriaticum

This is the leading homeopathic remedy for people suffering from the chronic effects of grief as a result of a broken rela-

tionship. The type of person who tends to need this remedy doesn't like consolation, avoids crying in the presence of others, and prefers to cry when alone. When they do cry, they cry in deep sobs.

☒ Pulsatilla

Consider this remedy when a person suffers from great indecision about relationships (and usually other things, too); when a person craves and needs sympathy of others during the breakup; and when a person cries (not sobs) in a sweet, gentle manner that beckons others to offer sympathy.

☒ Staphysagria

This remedy is indicated for people who have been physically or emotionally abused in a relationship. It is indicated when the person who is abused has suppressed the anger he or she has until it explodes. This remedy is also valuable when a person has experienced great humiliation.

BRUISES

Time is an honored treatment for bruises, but you can actually speed up the time in which healing takes place by using homeopathic remedies.

Use the 6th, 12th, or 30th potency every two hours in severe bruising, and four times a day in average bruising. It is rarely necessary to take a remedy longer than two days. You can also apply *Arnica* or *Calendula* externally in an ointment, gel, or spray at the same time you take an internal remedy. *Arnica* is fantastic for bruises without any cuts through the skin; while *Calendula* helps stop bleeding from cuts and wounds, and aids in their healing.

⚱ **Arnica (internal doses)**
This is the leading remedy to help the body absorb the blood under the skin in a bruise.

⚱ **Bellis perennis**
When a person suffers from a bruise to the abdomen or any deep bruise, consider this remedy.

⚱ **Ledum**
This is the leading remedy for a black eye. Also, when a bruise feels cold or numb and feels better after a cold application, use this remedy.

⚱ **Ruta**
For bone bruises, especially to the knee, elbow, or shin, this is the first remedy to consider.

BURNS

Homeopathic medicines can help lessen the pain from a burn and heal it as well. While second- and third-degree burns or extensive first-degree burns require medical attention, homeopathic remedies can be used concurrently.

Consider using internal and external applications to speed the healing of burns. External applications should be applied whenever a dressing is changed. When using a tincture, make certain to dilute it in at least three parts water so that the alcohol in the tincture doesn't burn the skin. Internal remedies should be given every two hours when there is severe pain and every four hours with most first-degree burns. Take these remedies only as long as pain from the burn exists. Don't forget to give several doses of *Arnica* in the 6th or 30th potency for second- or third-degree burns to help relieve the shock of injury.

✁ **Calendula
This external application in a gel, spray, or diluted tincture is recommended in first-degree burns.

✁ Hypericum
This remedy comes in both internal and external forms. Take it internally if there are any shooting pains or burns of the hands or feet. Apply it externally in a gel, spray, or diluted tincture in second-degree burns.

✁ Urtica urens
This is a great remedy for the pain of first-degree burns.

✁ Cantharis
This is an excellent remedy for relieving the pain of second- or third-degree burns.

✁ Phosphorus
If an electrical burn is experienced, use this remedy.

✁ Causticum
Consider this remedy if a burn does not heal well.

C

A flower in a laboratory flask represents the integration
of natural medicine and modern pharmacy

CANCER

Although many cancers are localized to a particular organ or part of the body, homeopaths understand cancer as a systemic disease, which requires the treatment of the entire person, not simply the localized disease. Homeopathy is uniquely useful in treating people with cancer because it is a powerful way to strengthen or tonify a person's immune system. Homeopathy is more successful in treating people with early-stage onset of cancer rather than at the end stages, though people with end-stage cancer may still experience some benefit from homeopathic remedies (but rarely a cure).

Homeopathy may be particularly useful after surgery has excised the cancer, and now the person needs something to strengthen their immune system to decrease the chance of a recurrence.

A book of this sort is unable to provide any specific remedies to treat people with cancer. Such treatment requires the care of a professional homeopath who provides a highly individualized remedy to an individual.

homeopathy a - z

homeopathy a - z

CANKER SORES

There are a couple of homeopathic remedies to consider in treating a person with canker sores, but because canker sores usually represent just one symptom of a person's overall complex of symptoms, the best remedy is sometimes something other than the three remedies below. In addition to considering homeopathy, a simple multiple vitamin can sometimes fill a nutritional deficiency and thereby provide necessary relief. You might also apply *Calendula* tincture or spray in the mouth and swish it around for 10 to 20 seconds.

Give the 6th or 12th potency one to three times.

**Borax

This is the leading remedy for canker sores. It is particularly indicated in children, especially when thrush is also active.

Calcarea carbonica

People who need this remedy tend to be overweight, have weak or flabby skin tone, suffer from indigestion, and sweat easily.

Mercurius

When a person experiences excessive saliva in the mouth alone with canker sores, consider this remedy.

CARPAL TUNNEL SYNDROME

This condition is best treated with a combination of internal and external homeopathic remedies. The external remedy should either be *Arnica* in an ointment or gel or a combination external remedy that includes *Arnica* along with several other remedies (there are numerous such products available in health food stores and in select pharmacies). Apply the external application at least two times a day. Apply it again if you wash it off when taking a bath or shower or when washing your hands. Internal remedies should be taken three to six times a day in the 6th, 12th, or 30th potency. If improvement isn't obvious after 48 hours, consider another remedy. In select cases, an individualized constitutional remedy may be necessary to complete the healing process.

☒ **Rhus toxicodendron
This is the most commonly indicated remedy for carpal tunnel syndrome. It is useful when the person experiences great pain upon initial motion and some relief upon continued motion. The person may also feel stiffness upon waking in the morning or after prolonged rest, and some aggravation of their symptoms in cold or wet weather.

☒ Causticum
When the wrist feels sprained and there is weakness, trembling, or any type of temporary paralysis, use this remedy.

☒ Bellis perennis
This remedy is indicated when there is pain "like a band around the wrist."

☒ Ruta
Consider this remedy if the wrist feels weak, lame, and stiff, or if the joint affected is the same as one that was injured a long time ago.

☒ Calcarea carbonica
This remedy tends to be indicated in people who are overweight, have lax skin tone, sweat easily, and have wrist pain as though they had sprained it.

homeopathy a-z

CHICKEN POX

Chicken pox can be a very mild ailment if the proper homeopathic medicines are used. Because homeopaths consider the common children's infectious diseases as useful in helping to strengthen their immune system, they usually recommend avoiding certain immunizations, especially for chicken pox, since it is not considered a severe ailment.

Give the 6th, 12th, or 30th potency of the remedy every other hour during the first day, and then four to six times a day while the child is still experiencing much itching. Once the irritation has stopped or has significantly been reduced, stop the remedy.

☒ **Rhus toxicodendron
This is by far the most commonly indicated remedy for chicken pox. It is useful when the child's condition is worsened by scratching, and more severe at night.

☒ Antimonium crudum
When the child has a honeylike discharge or thick, hardened, honey-colored scabs, this is the remedy to consider.

☒ Antimonium tarticum
If the child experiences a concurrent loose, rattling cough with their chicken pox, this remedy should be given.

☒ Croton tiglium
If the child's itching is intense and painful and the skin feels tight or "hide-bound," consider this remedy.

☒ Belladonna
A child who has a high fever that accompanies the skin rash should be given this remedy, especially if he or she has a flushed face, hot skin, drowsiness, and wild or scary dreams.

☒ Pulsatilla
When a child demands much attention and sympathy and is whiny and clingy, this remedy should be considered, especially if the itching is aggravated from warmth or from becoming overheated.

CHILDBIRTH

Childbirth is not a disease to be treated, but it is a condition that is stressful to the mother and child for which homeopathic remedies can be helpful. They can also strengthen the mother's uterus so that she can bear children more easily, decrease her bleeding and bruising, and reduce many complications of this powerful life-giving experience. Homeopathic remedies can complement any conventional medications that are given.

All homeopathic remedies given to the mother during pregnancy and childbirth will also benefit the fetus, and any that are given to the mother after childbirth will also be given to the newborn if breastfed.

It is impossible to list remedies for the various problems that may occur during childbirth. It is therefore recommended that readers augment the information provided here with other books on the subject.

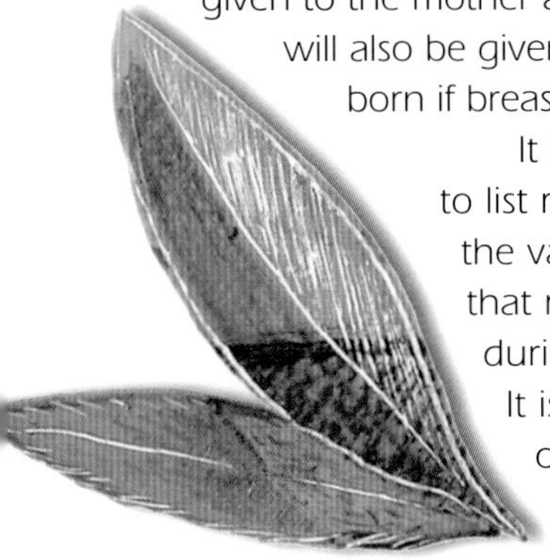

Give the 6th, 12th, or 30th potency every other hour during early stages of labor and every hour during intense labor.

**Arnica

This is the leading remedy to help reduce the shock and trauma of labor for the mother and newborn and will reduce uterine bleeding that may occur.

Caulophyllum

This remedy helps strengthen the women's uterine walls so that she can more easily push the child out into the world. It is particularly indicated when the woman experiences strong labor pains but is not dilating or is progressing extremely slowly. It is also indicated when the woman is more exhausted than one might expect at the stage of labor that she is in. Also, she may experience some muscular weakness, trembling, or twitching.

Cimicifuga

This remedy is important when the woman becomes very emotional (perhaps hysterical) and feels "she can't take it anymore." She may be exhibiting great fears about what bad things may happen during birth. She may also experience various physical symptoms, including headache, neuralgia (electric shocks felt anywhere), or arthritic pains in her hands.

☘ Pulsatilla

This remedy is very beneficial for many women, especially those who are very emotional, brought to tears easily, and desire sympathy. *Pulsatilla* is known to be great for helping to turn breech babies. It also helps steady a woman who is very emotional so that she can more effectively and easily give birth.

CIRCUMCISION

Doctors previously assumed that babies do not feel pain. We know otherwise today. Homeopathic remedies are not "painkillers" in the traditional sense of the word, but they do help the baby heal from this physically and psychologically traumatic experience more rapidly, and because of this, they reduce the intensity and the length of the pain the baby feels.

Give the 12th or 30th potency of the remedy once just prior to the surgery, every hour after the first three doses, and every other hour for the rest of the day. Give it two to four times on the second day.

♉ Arnica
This remedy will help reduce the shock and trauma of the surgical procedure. It is recommended just before and immediately after circumcision.

♉ Staphysagria
After the first three to six doses of *Arnica*, give *Staphysagria* since it is a leading remedy for stab wounds.

♉ Calendula
An external application of this remedy in an ointment, gel, or spray may help the penis heal.

COLD SORES
(Herpes Simplex)

Homeopathic remedies have an impressive history of successful treatment of viral conditions. Although homeopathic self-care may reduce the intensity of a herpes eruption, professional homeopathic care is necessary if a person wants to reduce the frequency of these eruptions.

Give the 6th, 12th, or 30th potency every 4 hours for up to 48 hours. Stop if significant improvement takes place before this time.

♉ **Natrum muriaticum
This is the most commonly given homeopathic medicine for herpes. It is particularly indicated for people with dry and cracked lips and for people who experience cold sores during various acute infections (the common cold, influenza, sore throat, etc.).

When an eruption occurs after prolonged exposure to the sun, this remedy is commonly indicated. If there is any fluid in the blister, it is a clear fluid.

(Cold Sores, cont'd.)

♓ **Rhus toxicodendron

This is another commonly given remedy for the acute phase of herpes simplex. It is indicated when there are small, inflamed blisters that appear in a cluster; usually with yellow, watery fluid.

♓ Hepar sulphuris

When the herpes is extremely sensitive to touch and to extremes of temperature, and when the person also becomes hypersensitive and irritable, consider this remedy.

♓ Arsenicum

This remedy is indicated when the eruption burns but feels relief from the application of warmth. This remedy is also useful in people who are restless and anxious, fastidious and demanding, and chilly and thirsty (but for only sips at a time).

COLIC

Homeopathic medicines are wonderfully effective in treating this all-too-common ailment of babies. Although doctors do not tend to understand what colic is, homeopaths and those who use these natural medicines know that homeopathic remedies significantly reduce the frequency and intensity of colic. What a blessing!

Give the 6th, 12th, or 30th potency of the remedy every hour for the first three doses, and every other hour afterwards. If relief isn't obvious after 12 hours, consider another remedy.

♓ **Chamomilla

This is by far the most effective remedy for colic. It is indicated in irritable infants who demand one thing or another but refuse it when it is offered. They are in great pain, and nothing provides any relief except being held and carried. However, this relief is temporary, for once the child is put down, he or she tends to cry again. The child tends to be worse at night and has one cheek red and hot and the other cheek pale and cold (this suggests a problem with teething).

⚱ Colocynthis

When an infant is extremely irritable, and firm pressure on the abdomen or painful area provides noticeable relief, this is the remedy to give. Warmth and having the baby bend over may also provide some relief.

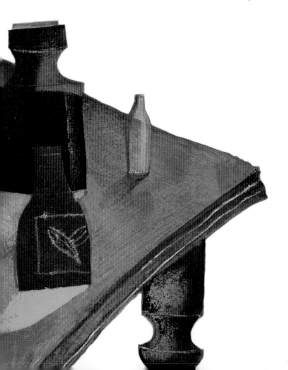

⚱ Magnesium phosphorica

Babies who are noticeably relieved by warmth or by bending double tend to benefit from this medicine. These babies tend to have much bloating, with loud burping and passing of gas.

⚱ Nux vomica

When breastfeeding mothers drink too much alcohol or take drugs (therapeutic or recreational), consider this remedy for their colicky infant.

⚱ Ignatia

If the breastfeeding mother has experienced great grief, give this remedy to the mother and the infant.

⚱ Aethusa

Consider this remedy in babies who are intolerant of milk and who vomit large curds shortly after milk is consumed. They may also have a profuse, cold sweat over their body.

COMMON COLD

It is no wonder that conventional medicine hasn't cured the common cold, since the drugs that are used primarily suppress a person's nasal discharge and weaken a person's ability to expel the dead viruses and white blood cells.

Instead, homeopathic medicines are prescribed for their ability to mimic the similar symptoms that the sick person is experiencing and therefore help them heal faster. Homeopathic medicines are wonderfully effective in treating this simple condition.

Give the 6th, 12th, or 30th potency every other hour during the first two or three doses, and then every fourth hour until the person is noticeably better. If improvement hasn't occurred after a single night's rest, consider another remedy. Besides the following remedies, consider one of the homeopathic combination remedies for colds when you can't figure out the individualized medicine or if it isn't immediately available.

♆ Aconitum

Good only for colds during the first 24 hours, this remedy is effective when symptoms come on suddenly, especially after exposure to cold. A dry cough and great thirst may also be concurrent.

♆ Oscillococcinum

This remedy is one of homeopathy's most popular cold and flu remedies, but it is important to know that it is primarily effective when used during the first 48 hours after onset. Consider this remedy when no other one is obviously indicated or immediately available.

Allium cepa

Made from the onion, this remedy is known to cause and cure symptoms that include a fluent and sometimes burning nasal discharge that irritates the nostrils, fluent tearing from the eyes, and frequent sneezing, all of which are worse in warm or stuffy rooms.

Arsenicum

Consider this remedy when a person has a burning, irritating, watery nasal discharge that is usually worse on the right side, and the person is more chilly than normal. These people are aggravated from being outside and being exposed to cold. Another characteristic symptom is that the person has a great thirst but prefers to drink only sips at a time.

Belladonna

When a cold has a sudden onset and is accompanied by a high fever (over 102 degrees), flushed red face, and a reddened sore throat, think of this remedy. Characteristically, the person tends to have glassy eyes and dilated pupils.

Kali bichromicum

If a person has a nasal discharge that is thick and stringy, consider this remedy. This person may also have a postnasal drip and pain at the root of the nose.

homeopathy a-z

♟ Pulsatilla

This remedy is often given to children and those people who tend to be weepy, clingy, and desirous of sympathy during their ill state. Typically, it is indicated in people who have thick yellow or greenish mucus and who experience an aggravation of symptoms in warm, stuffy rooms and at night. These people strongly prefer to keep windows open to help breathe fresh, cool air. Lack of thirst is also very common.

♟ Nux vomica

This remedy should be considered when a person experiences a runny nose during the day and in warm rooms, and a stuffy nose at night and indoors. Typically, symptoms of a cold may start either after exposure to cold or after overeating, overdrinking (alcohol), or abuse of recreational drugs.

64

homeopathy a-z

CONJUNCTIVITIS

Bacterial infection or an allergy can cause this condition commonly called "pinkeye." Scientific research has shown that homeopathic remedies can effectively treat allergic conjunctivitis, although clinical experience has also confirmed positive results in treating bacterial conjunctivitis. One can generally expect rapid results with homeopathic remedies, usually leading to resolution after a single night's rest.

Give the 6th, 12th, or 30th potency every other hour for the first two doses and every four hours after that. If improvement is not observed after 24 hours, consider another remedy.

☧ Pulsatilla

This is the most common remedy for this condition. When a person experiences a thick yellow or yellow-greenish discharge from the eye that doesn't irritate the skin but may lead to itching or burning of the eye itself, especially in the evening, consider this remedy. Cold applications or being in the open air may provide some relief. Other indications for using this remedy are people who exhibit the known personality characteristics of this remedy: being emotional, weepy, clingy, and desirous of sympathy.

☧ Apis

This remedy should be taken when there is great swelling and puffiness of the eyelids as well as redness, which is aggravated by heat and relieved by cool applications.

☧ Belladonna

Consider this remedy when there is sudden onset, the eye feels hot, looks red, may throb, and light irritates the eye.

☧ Euphrasia

This remedy is indicated when there is a profuse flow of acrid tears that may burn the lower lid and cheek.

☧ Mercurius

People who need this remedy experience a yellow or yellow-greenish discharge from the eye that is irritating to the skin. Eye discharge and pain are aggravated at night, by the warmth of the bed, and by light.

homeopathy a - z

COUGHS

Books on physiology and pathology typically refer to the body's cough reflex as an important defensive function of the organism, yet many conventional cough medicines are known to suppress the cough. While such medicines provide temporary relief, they tend to prolong the ailment, and still worse, they tend to lead to various side effects that create their own problems.

Homeopathic remedies are wonderfully effective in treating people with coughs; however, it is sometimes difficult to find the correct remedy if a person doesn't have many differentiating symptoms. If this is the case, consider taking one of the homeopathic combination remedies for coughs that are available at health food stores or pharmacies. When available, find a product that more precisely describes your cough, as in "dry cough" or "congestive cough."

Give the 6th, 12th, or 30th potency every other hour in extreme cases for two doses, and every four hours after this. If relief isn't noticeable after 48 hours, consider another remedy.

Aconitum
Consider this remedy during the first 24 hours of a dry or croupy cough, especially if it starts after exposure to cold or after an experience of fright.

Spongia
This remedy is indicated for dry, loud, frequent, croupy coughs, when the cough may even sound like a sawing of a log. The cough is aggravated by talking, cold drinks, or getting excited, and is usually worse before or after midnight.

Bryonia
When a person has a dry cough that is aggravated by motion of the chest of

any kind (inspiration, especially deep breathing, talking, or eating), consider this remedy. Motion of the chest can be so painful that they may even place their hands over their chest to inhibit chest motion. They prefer to lie still, remain as motionless as possible, and be left alone due to their increasing irritability.

☿ Rumex

A dry cough that is aggravated when the person lies down to rest or sleep suggests the use of this medicine. Typically, this person experiences a tickle in the pit of the throat that aggravates the cough and may create a fit of coughing. The cough, which may become continual, is worse when breathing in cold air, lying on the left side, and when touching the throat.

☿ Phosphorus

When chills and laryngitis or hoarseness accompany a cough, this remedy should be considered, especially when there is a great thirst for cold, icy water to drink. The cough is aggravated by cold air, talking, lying on the back or left side, or exposure to strong odors.

☿ Hepar sulphuris

This medicine is for people during the later stages of a dry cough when there may be rattling in the chest but an inability to expectorate mucus. These people are hypersensitive to cold and cold air, to eating or drinking anything cold, and they are also emotionally hypersensitive and even hyper-irritable.

☿ Pulsatilla

This is a common cough remedy for children and others who have the characteristic symptoms of being emotional, weepy, clingy, and desirous of sympathy. Typically, people who need this remedy have a thick yellow or yellow-green expectoration; and their cough is worse after eating, lying down at night, and being in a warm or stuffy room.

☿ Antimonium tartaricum

This is the premier remedy for a loose, rattling cough, although the person is not easily able to expectorate. It is commonly indicated for children and the elderly. Usually, the person wishes to be left alone and may experience great sleepiness during the illness.

☒ Coccus cacti
This remedy should be considered when there is an accumulation of thick, stringy mucus in the throat and nose that causes the person to constantly try to clear the throat. A fit of coughing may ensue. They experience a great thirst for cold drinks that provide short-term relief for them.

☒ Ipecacuahna
When vomiting and/or nausea are concurrent with a cough, consider this remedy. Typically, the cough is loose, and the person may have a nosebleed or some other type of bleeding problem (blood in the expectoration).

homeopathy a - z

CUTS AND SCRAPES

Time can and will heal cuts and scrapes, but homeopathic medicines can and will speed the healing process. The use of external homeopathic remedies are recommended for all cuts and scrapes, while internal remedies are only necessary if there is significant pain or discomfort.

External applications are made in various forms: ointment, gel, tincture, or spray. If a tincture is used, dilute it in water so that its alcohol doesn't burn. Reapply external applications after every bathing. When necessary, give the 6th, 12th, or 30th potency every four hours for up to two days.

🏺 **Calendula (external)
This is the leading remedy for cuts and scrapes, as long as the cut isn't too deep. After a deep cut begins to heal, apply this remedy to speed up the final healing.

🏺 Hypericum (external)
This is the leading remedy for deep cuts.

🏺 Arnica (internal)
Use this remedy if there is considerable pain or discomfort.

🏺 Hypericum (internal)
Use this remedy if there are sharp or shooting pains from the injury.

🏺 Ledum (internal)
Use this remedy for puncture wounds.

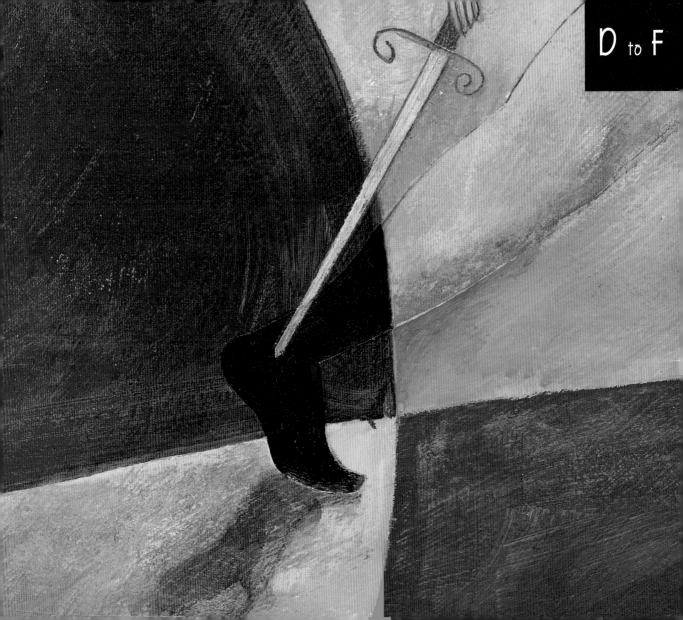

D to F

Even powerful
warriors such as
Achilles have their
weaknesses. Out of
these weaknesses we
learn about our limitations.

DEPRESSION

Depression can be a temporary, passing experience or a deeply disturbing condition that leads to suicide. Except in cases of minor and temporary depression, professional attention is generally recommended to help a person go through this emotional experience in a conscious manner.

Homeopathic remedies can also help a person pass through depressive states in a healthy way. Charles Frederick Menninger, M.D., the founder of the Menninger Clinic, which is one of the most famous mental health institutions in the world, was originally a homeopath and was known to assert that homeopathy is instrumental in helping people heal from various physical and psychological traumas.

A book of this nature can only highlight a limited number of remedies. Seek other homeopathic guidebooks for information on other remedies.

Give the 30th potency every two hours for the first couple of doses, and every four hours after that. It is rarely necessary to have to take remedies for depression longer than a couple of days. If there is no relief by then, consider another remedy, or seek professional homeopathic attention.

☗ **Ignatia
This is the leading remedy for acute grief, especially after the loss of a loved one, the breakup of a relationship, the loss of a job, or an experience of abuse. Typically, the person who needs this remedy tries to hold in his or her emotions, but eventually, hysterical sobbing occurs. Frequent sighing is a keynote characteristic of people who require *Ignatia*.

☒ Pulsatilla

This remedy is for people who weep easily, are openly emotional, are extremely clingy, strongly desire sympathy and consolation, tend to be dependent upon others, and feel forsaken. People who need this remedy do not sob, but instead experience a type of sweet crying that inspires others to hug them, which is exactly what these people want and need.

☒ Staphysagria

People who need this remedy have probably gone through great humiliation. They experience low self-esteem, and they are no longer able to hold in their emotions. In this process, they feel depression and anger. They blame themselves and lash out at whoever hurt them.

☒ Natrum muriaticum

People who benefit from this remedy tend to be stoic, holding in and not revealing their emotions. They rarely cry in front of others, and they hate to receive sympathy or consolation from others. When alone, however, they can and will sob uncontrollably. These people hold grudges for a long time.

DIAPER RASH

Diaper rash is a skin irritation or infection that results from prolonged contact of a soiled diaper with a baby's skin. Diaper rash can also result from an allergy to certain laundry detergents used on cloth diapers, or certain chemicals in disposable diapers.

The best "treatment" for diaper rash is frequent changing of a baby's diaper. Homeopathic medicines can also be used to soothe and nourish the baby's skin to make it more resistant to irritation, infection, or allergy.

The best homeopathic medicine for diaper rash is an external application, which should be applied at least twice daily or at least after every washing.

☒ **Calendula (external)

Made from marigolds, this remedy is full of carotenoids that nourish the skin; and organic iodine, which helps to fight infection.

☒ Candida albicans

If diaper rash is caused by a yeast infection, consider taking the 30th potency of this remedy twice a day for no longer than two days.

☒ Sulphur

If neither of the above remedies work well enough, and if there is much redness and irritation, consider this remedy in the 6th or 30th potency twice a day for no longer than two days at a time.

DIARRHEA (acute)

Diarrhea is one of the important defenses of the body. It is the way that the body hastens elimination of certain infectious organisms. Although one can consider taking conventional drugs to suppress the diarrhea, they simply allow the bacteria or parasites to remain in the body longer.

The World Health Organization considers childhood diarrhea to be the number-one public health problem in the world today, as it can lead to dehydration, which causes over five million children in the world to die each year.

Scientific studies have verified the value of homeopathic remedies to treat acute diarrhea in children. One does not need to be a professional homeopath to learn to use these remedies for acute diarrhea.

Give the 6th, 12th, or 30th potency after every bowel movement. At first, this will lead to more frequent doses, but as the person improves, decreasing doses will be necessary. Stop once the person has normal, firm stools.

🏺 **Podophyllum

This remedy is the leading one for diarrhea. It is indicated when the person experiences a sudden urgency to release a stool (it may even drive the person out of bed early in the morning); and when there are profuse, offensive-smelling stools and great rumbling and gurgling in the abdomen before the stool release. Typically, the release of the stool is painless. People who need this remedy tend to have a great thirst for cold liquids.

🏺 **Arsenicum

This remedy is the leading one for diarrhea caused by food poisoning or viral diseases. The diarrhea is worse after eating or drinking; and nausea, vomiting, and burning or cramping pains in the abdomen may accompany the diarrhea. People usually become exhausted by the diarrhea, but they are also restless, fidgety, and generally anxious. They may have a fever with chills, and whether they do or not, they are very sensitive to cold. They can be very thirsty but can only handle drinking sips of fluids at a time.

🏺 Aloe socotrina

When people experience a distinct feeling of insecurity in the rectum that may lead to accidental expelling of a stool after passing gas, this remedy should be considered. The stools themselves are very mucusy and like Jell-o. The person may concurrently experience hemorrhoids.

🏺 Veratrum album

People who experience profuse, painful diarrhea that is forcibly evacuated followed by great weakness should consider this remedy. Despite feeling very chilly, these people crave ice and cold drinks. People who tend to have profuse sweating with chills should consider this remedy.

☒ Chamomilla

This remedy is useful in infants who experience diarrhea, especially when they are extremely irritable during their illness. Typically, the diarrhea is foul smelling and green, or has white or yellow mucus. The infants are in great pain, and holding and carrying them is the only thing that provides relief (and this is temporary).

☒ Calcarea carbonica

Like *Chamomilla*, this remedy is more commonly given to infants. It is particularly common in infants with a lot of baby fat, who are pale and lethargic, and who emit a sour odor from their body and sweat profusely, especially on the head. They tend to crave eggs and indigestible things (chalk, dirt).

DRUG ADDICTION

The treatment of drug addiction requires professional homeopathic care. Such treatment can help people who are addicted to either recreational or therapeutic (conventional) drugs. Homeopathy can help reduce cravings, decrease the side effects of the drugs and of the withdrawal process, augment the detoxification process, and aid in the recovery of the person's overall health.

EARACHES

Earaches have become so common in American children that they are the number-one reason parents take their child to a physician today. One of the factors contributing to this recurring problem is that antibiotics may reduce the infection, but they tend to increase the chances for return of the ear problem.

Homeopathic remedies are wonderfully effective in treating this common ailment. Although recurrent or severe earaches may require the care of a professional homeopath, there are several homeopathic remedies that people can use at home to heal acute earaches.

Give the 6th, 12th, or 30th potency every other hour during intense pain, and every four hours when there's mild discomfort. Relief is commonly experienced within a couple of hours or after a night's rest. If a child still has pain 24 hours after a homeopathic remedy has been given, consider giving another remedy or seek professional homeopathic attention.

♟ Belladonna

This remedy is useful for earaches that start suddenly; when the child has intense, throbbing ear pain; or when the child has a bright red outer ear or ear canal. This type of earache is often accompanied by a high fever. These children are sensitive to light, noise, or being jarred. Children who need this remedy tend to be delirious during sleep and have nightmares, usually about animals, which cause them to cry out.

♟ Pulsatilla

This remedy is indicated when the child becomes whiny and extremely clingy, wants to be hugged and cuddled, has pain worse at night and in a warm room, and usually has little or no thirst. The child who needs this remedy tends

to have a changeable mood, happy and playing one minute and crying and sad the next. In advanced cases, there may be a thick yellow or green discharge from the ear or nose.

✷ Chamomilla

When the child with an earache becomes hyper-irritable, extremely fussy, aggravated by touch or by bending or stooping over, and is temporarily relieved by being cradled and rocked, consider this remedy. This remedy is also useful for infants with an earache who are concurrently teething.

✷ Hepar sulphuris

This remedy is useful for hyper-irritable children who are hypersensitive to any type of touch or exposure to cold. Their earache may be accompanied by a thick discharge from their ear or nose and may have ear pain that extends to the throat.

✷ Mercurius

Children who have an earache that is sensitive to extremes of heat and cold temperature and who experience profuse sweating at night often benefit from this remedy. They also tend to have increased salivation

at night in bed, swollen tonsils and lymph glands, and noticeably offensive bad breath.

homeopathy a–z

FATIGUE

Fatigue is not a disease itself, but a symptom of disease. Except for simple fatigue, which is the result of exhaustion, most people with fatigue have a condition that results from a multifactorial assortment of causes, including lifestyle issues, viral infection, genetic predisposition, and previous suppressive conventional medical treatment. Homeopathic remedies can be wonderfully effective in treating people with acute or chronic fatigue, but generally it requires the care of a professional homeopath.

FEARS AND PHOBIAS

Homeopathy has an impressive history of effective treatment of people with various fears and phobias. Due to the diversity and complexity of fears and phobias, they require professional homeopathic care rather than self-care.

There are, however, a couple of simple homeopathic remedies to consider for specific types of situations related to fear. Use the 6th, 12th, or 30th potency every other hour for the first couple of doses. After this, you can take a couple more, four hours apart for a day or two if necessary.

⚗ Aconitum
When people experience fear after an accident, injury, or traumatic natural event (earthquake, tornado, hurricane, fire, etc.) and feel like they may die or that they are in real trouble, this remedy can help them regain a sense of calm.

☒ Arnica

People who experience fear after an injury and who want to be left alone will benefit from this remedy.

☒ Gelsemium

People who develop stage fright or anticipatory anxiety and whose mind goes blank prior to a performance or an examination can benefit from taking this remedy.

☒ Argentum nitricum

This remedy can help people who develop stage fright or anticipatory anxiety prior to a performance or an examination and who experience diarrhea and/or flatulence as a result.

☒ Stramonium

When people have a combined fear of animals (even dogs), a fear of water, and a fear of the dark, this remedy should be considered.

FEVER

Conventional physicians have finally recognized that fever is an important defense of the body. Fevers are the way that the body tries to heat up and burn out bacterial and viral infection. If one takes an aspirin or other drug that suppresses the fever, it can lead to unpleasant, sometimes serious side effects, especially in children and in people who are immuno-compromised.

Homeopathic medicines help strengthen the body so that it can fight infection more effectively. Use the 6th, 12th, or 30th potency every other hour in fevers of 102 or higher, and every four hours when there are lower fevers. It is rarely necessary to have to take a homeopathic remedy for longer than 36 hours. If a person has a fever of 102 or higher, the remedy will usually provide a benefit within two hours. If it doesn't, you can consider using another, or seek professional attention. See the section on influenza for additional fever remedies.

Aconitum
This remedy is primarily useful during the first 24 hours of a fever. It is helpful when a fever begins after exposure to cold or cold, dry winds. Chilliness and a cold sweat may also be experienced.

Belladonna
When a person has a rapid onset of a high fever with a flushed face, reddened mucus membranes, glassy eyes, and cold limbs, consider this remedy. Typically, the person tends to have wild dreams at night.

Oscillococcinum
This is a wonderful remedy for fevers when you don't know of any other one to use. The trick to this remedy is that you must use it within the first 48 hours of onset of a fever.

Nux vomica
When a fever with chills begins after an overindulgence of food, drink (alcohol), or drug use, consider this remedy.

FIBROMYALGIA
(fibrositis)

This chronic musculoskeletal syndrome is becoming increasingly common, especially among women. One important study showed that homeopathic remedies were effective in providing relief for this condition. This study found that 42 percent of people with this ailment benefited from *Rhus toxicodendron*. Although this remedy and others mentioned below will often be effective in providing short-term relief, it is recommended that one seek professional homeopathic care to obtain deeper, longer-term relief.

Use the 6th, 12th, or 30th potency every two hours during intense pain syndromes, and every four hours during less intense times. Take doses as little as possible but as much as necessary. If improvement isn't noticed within 24 hours, consider another remedy.

**Rhus toxicodendron
This remedy is indicated when the person has symptoms similar to that of a rusty

gate—that is, the pain is worse upon initial motion but is relieved by continued motion. Pain is also worse during rest after prolonged motion; at night in bed; and in cold, wet weather.

☒ Bryonia

This remedy is valuable when people experience pain as a result of any type of motion. They feel some temporary relief when firm pressure is applied to the painful area. Psychologically, they are very irritable and insist upon being alone.

☒ Pulsatilla

When the person experiences pain in areas of the body that constantly change from one place to another, this remedy should be considered. Typically, there is some relief when the person is exposed to cold, and some aggravation of symptoms at night or when one is exposed to warmth or heat.

FLU
(see Influenza)

FOOD POISONING
(see Diarrhea, Indigestion, and Nausea and Vomiting)

FRACTURES

Fractures require medical attention to set the bones, but they can also benefit from the concurrent use of homeopathic remedies to help speed bone healing.

Use the 6th, 12th, or 30th potency six times a day during the first day and four times a day for up to one week. After this, take one dose per week.

In addition to using the remedies below for bone healing, it is important to take *Arnica* in the 6th, 12th, or 30th potency during the first day to help deal with the shock and trauma of the injury.

☒ Symphytum
This is the most important remedy to help in the healing of fractures. It is also useful for fractures that are slow to heal.

☒ Ruta
When the bone is extremely sore, this remedy helps to reduce the pain and heal the bone.

☒ Calcarea phosphorica
When bones do not heal after a long time, this remedy should be considered.

FRIGHT
(see Fears and Phobias)

G to H

Snake venoms are powerful and wonderful medicine (in homeopathic doses!

HAY FEVER
(see Allergies)

HEADACHES

Conventional medicine is relatively effective in providing short-term relief from the pain of headaches; however, there is the price of short- and long-term side effects attendant to these conventional drugs. Homeopathic remedies provide a safer alternative.

Use the 6th, 12th, or 30th potency every other hour when there is intense pain, and every four hours for the average pain associated with a headache. Consider another remedy if there is no improvement after three doses.

☒ Belladonna
This is a leading remedy for intense, throbbing headaches that are aggravated by light, noise, touch, motion, simple jarring (even the person's hair is sensitive to touch), and lying down. The head pains tend to be relieved by sitting in a semi-erect position, using cold applications, and applying firm pressure. It is indicated for headaches, especially right-sided ones, that come and go and then return suddenly. Commonly, the person's face is flushed or hot, and their pupils are dilated.

☒ Bryonia
When a person has such bursting and splitting pain that simple motion of any kind, even moving the eyes, aggravates the headache, consider this remedy. The pains are typically in the front part of the head and are relieved by firm pressure. The head pains tend to be accompanied by indigestion and/or constipation. People who need *Bryonia* tend to be irritable and insist upon being alone.

☒ Nux vomica
Headaches associated with overeating, overdrinking (alcohol), coffee consumption, or drug use are often effectively treat-

ed with this remedy. The headache is typically worse upon waking up and is relieved by being in a warm room, sitting quietly, and lying down. Great irritability and constipation with a headache is common with people who need this remedy.

Gelsemium

Head pains in the back of the head and headaches associated with dimness of vision or some other type of visual disturbances are often treated with this remedy. The head pains are aggravated from lying with the head low, from exposure to the heat of the sun, and from mental exertion, while the pains tend to be relieved after profuse urination. People who benefit from this remedy tend to be extremely fatigued, have apathetic feelings, and are usually without thirst. Also, this remedy is useful for people who get a headache prior to or after some type of performance or test.

Sanguinaria

This remedy often provides relief for people with right-sided migraines, usually over the right eye, especially when they also suffer from indigestion with a burning pain in the abdomen. This is a common remedy for headaches in women during menopause.

Spigelia

People with left-sided headaches, even affecting their face, benefit from this remedy. They may feel a lot of pain in their left eye socket and are aggravated by motion.

Coffea

A headache concurrent with insomnia is typical of people who fit the need for this remedy. Also, use this remedy for headaches related to coffee consumption.

homeopathy a-z

HEAD INJURIES

Ailments stemming from a head injury can be either minor or major. Homeopaths have affirmed good results using homeopathic remedies for various ailments after head injuries, and now some new research has confirmed these positive clinical experiences.

Use the 6th, 12th, or 30th potency every other hour during the first day after an injury, and four times a day after then. If improvement is not obvious after 48 hours, consider another remedy.

☒ **Arnica
This is the first remedy to consider to help deal with the shock and trauma of a head injury and to prevent long-term problems from it.

☒ Belladonna
When there is much heat, redness, throbbing, and fullness in the head after an injury, consider this remedy. The person may become delirious, frantic, and may bite or strike at those around him or her.

☒ Hypericum
Consider this remedy if there are sharp and shooting pains or if there are spasms or seizures after a head injury.

☒ Cicuta
If the person experiences seizures after a head injury or if a head injury is severe enough to suggest mental retardation, consider this remedy.

homeopathy a-z

☒ Natrum sulphur

This remedy is useful when a person has long-term symptoms after a head injury, even when the symptoms may not be in the head. This remedy is also indicated when the person develops suicidal thoughts.

☒ Hellaborus

If a person develops severe mental dullness and very slow talking after a head injury, think of this remedy.

HEART DISEASE

Heart disease is serious enough to warrant the attention of a professional homeopath. Homeopathy should be considered in conjunction with various lifestyle changes, exercise, herbal remedies, nutritional supplements, group support, and medical monitoring.

There is no simple treatment or small number of common homeopathic remedies for people with heart disease. There are literally hundreds of possible remedies that can be beneficial.

HEMORRHOIDS

Homeopathic remedies are wonderful treatments for hemorrhoids, although it is also recommended that the person add more fiber to their diet and more exercise to their lifestyle.

In addition to the remedies below, it is sometimes helpful to concurrently use one of the homeopathic hemorrhoidal external applications that are available at select health food stores.

Use the 6th, 12th, or 30th potency three times a day for up to three days.

☒ **Aesculus

This is the leading homeopathic remedy for hemorrhoids, especially when the hemorrhoids feel like a splinter or a stick, and it feels as though the rectum is protruding outside the anus. The person may also have a sense of fullness after releasing a stool and an aching in the lower back or base of the spine. Pain from the hemorrhoid is usually worse from touch and after a bowel movement. This is an important remedy for women with hemorrhoids during menopause.

☸ Aloe socotrina

Consider this remedy when a person feels a sense of insecurity as though a stool will be released by accident, and after passing gas. People who need this remedy tend to have rectal discomfort that may wake them up in the morning.

☸ Hamamelis

This is a remedy for bleeding hemorrhoids with much soreness, rawness, and itching of the rectum. Generally, the person's stools are hard and tend to be coated with mucus.

☸ Belladonna

During the early onset of hemorrhoids, consider this remedy when there is acute inflammation; much redness, swelling, and tenderness; and bright, red blood.

☸ Collinsonia

This remedy is indicated when the person has chronic constipation that alternates with diarrhea. It is also indicated when the person has swelling in the face or lips concurrently with the hemorrhoids.

☸ Nux vomica

This remedy is useful in people who have a tendency to overeat, overdrink (alcohol), and overindulge in drugs (recreational or therapeutic). The person who needs this remedy tends to have frequent, ineffectual urges for a bowel movement, despite much straining. These people are usually very irritable.

HEPATITIS (acute)

People with chronic or severe hepatitis should seek professional homeopathic care. Most people with acute hepatitis can often benefit from one of the homeopathic remedies listed below.

Use the 6th, 12th, or 30th potency three times a day for three days, but if there is no obvious change after two days, consider another remedy.

☒ **Chelidonium
This is the most common remedy for people with acute hepatitis. The person's liver is enlarged and sensitive to touch, and there may be pain in the liver, extending backwards. The person feels generally lethargic, heavy-headed, and chilly.

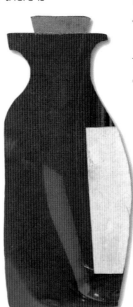

☒ Lycopodium
When a person with hepatitis experiences so much bloating that they can't tolerate tight clothing around their abdomen, consider this remedy. The person's symptoms are typically worse between 4 and 8 P.M. and after eating (they tend to feel full or bloated even after ingesting small amounts).

☒ Nux vomica
This is a leading remedy for hepatitis and other liver problems that are in part the result of alcoholism or drug abuse (recreational or therapeutic drugs).

☒ Mercurius
When a person has offensive, profuse sweating; bad breath; and a coated, swollen tongue that easily takes the imprint from one's teeth, consider this remedy. Typically, these people are sensitive to both hot and cold and feel worse at night.

☒ Phosphorus

Think of this remedy if and when a person with hepatitis has great thirst and craves ice or carbonated drinks.

HERPES
(see Cold Sores)

HIVES

Hives is an allergic condition that responds very rapidly to homeopathic medicines. Recurrent attacks of hives are best treated by a professional homeopath.

Use the 6th, 12th, or 30th potency every two hours. If improvement isn't obvious after three doses, consider another remedy.

☒ **Apis

This is the most common remedy for hives. It is especially indicated when the hives include swelling, redness, and heat; are aggravated by exposure to warmth; and are relieved by exposure to cold. Typically, people who benefit from this remedy develop hives at night or during or after exercise.

☒ Urtica urens

This is another common remedy for hives. Its characteristic symptoms include hives that are burning and itching and are aggravated by bathing or warmth, and which are relieved by lying down or rubbing the affected parts.

☒ Rhus toxicodendron

When hives are itching and are aggravated by scratching, consider this remedy.

☒ Histiminium

If you don't know which remedy to use or if the indicated remedy isn't working, consider *Histiminium*.

homeopathy a–z

A mortar and pestle are vita
tools for awakening the healin
properties of our medicine.

INDIGESTION

Indigestion refers to a wide variety of digestive complaints, including heartburn, abdominal bloating, gas, eructation (burping), nausea, and vomiting. Many people incorrectly assume that such symptoms are the result of nutritional problems. While this is certainly true some of the time, indigestion can also be the result of various disease processes that reduce the ability of a person to digest and assimilate their foods. Indigestion can also be influenced by strong emotions that are felt during or shortly after eating.

There is also a tendency for some people to think that they are allergic to a specific food that is causing their indigestion. It is certainly possible for this to happen, and a simple way to evaluate if this is true is to take that food out of one's diet and to carefully monitor one's symptoms. Some foods, such as corn, soy, or wheat, are difficult to eliminate from the diet because many processed foods include by-products of these foods.

Homeopathic remedies can help improve a person's digestive process in the short and long term. However, long-term improvement generally requires professional homeopathic care, while the following remedies tend to provide short-term relief. (Also see the section on "Nausea and Vomiting" later in this book.)

Take the 6th, 12th, or 30th potency every two hours for two or three doses during intense discomfort, and three times a day when there are mild symptoms. If no obvious improvement occurs within 24 hours, try another remedy. Consider seeking professional homeopathic care if symptoms are severe, persistent, or recurring.

☒ Arsenicum

This is a leading remedy for indigestion when people feel burning pains in the stomach or rectum, a great thirst but for only sips at a time, chilliness with an aggravation from exposure to cold, a general restlessness, and anxiety about one's health. These individuals experience an aggravation of their symptoms at midnight and afterwards.

☒ Pulsatilla

Commonly given to children and women, this remedy is good for indigestion or heartburn after one eats fatty food (ice cream, fried food) or pork; or when one has a lack of thirst, an aversion to stuffy rooms, and a desire for open air. Typically, someone with these symptoms is highly emotional and craves sympathy and attention.

☒ Ipecacuanha

This is a leading remedy for nausea and vomiting, especially when the nausea is persistent, even after vomiting. Other characteristic symptoms include a lack of thirst, increased salivation, and an uncoated tongue.

☒ Nux vomica

Digestive problems that start after overeating; overconsumption of alcohol, coffee, or drugs (therapeutic or recreational); or mental stress are commonly relieved by this remedy. Heartburn, nausea, and gas are usually accompanied with increased irritability and usually a headache, all of which tend to be worse in the morning upon waking up. This is the leading homeopathic remedy for people with a hangover

☒ Bryonia

People who feel digestive discomfort after any type of motion could benefit from this remedy. People who need this remedy tend to be constipated, irritable, want to be alone, and have a great thirst for cold liquids. Typically, these people have a feeling of pressure in their stomach, as though there was a stone there, and they feel nauseated and faint upon sitting up or standing.

☒ Lycopodium

This is a leading remedy for people who experience bloating, gas, and belching. People who need this remedy have an abdomen that is sensitive to any pressure, whether it is from a belt or elastic waist-band. Typically, their symptoms are worse between 4 and 8 P.M. People who benefit from this remedy tend to crave sweets and often feel full after eating only a small amount of food, although this doesn't always stop them from eating.

☒ Sulphur

People with heartburn from overeating or eating the wrong foods and who may also suffer from early-morning diarrhea often benefit from this remedy. Typically, these people tend to feel generalized heat from their body that makes exposure to cool or cold air feel good and leads to an aggravation of symptoms from warmth or heat.

INFLUENZA

When a fever is accompanied by headache, aching muscles, sore throat, cough, nasal congestion, fever and chills, and generalized fatigue, it is most likely that the person is infected with one of the many influenza viruses. In addition to these symptoms, some people may also experience various digestive complaints, including nausea, vomiting, diarrhea, and gas.

Conventional medicine offers nothing for such viral conditions, but homeopathic medicines are wonderfully effective in restoring a person back to health, and several scientific studies have confirmed this.

Use the 6th, 12th, or 30th potency every other hour for the first two or three doses, and then every six to eight hours until resolution of the condition occurs. If significant improvement doesn't occur after 24 hours, consider another remedy.

☤ Oscillococcinum

This remedy is effective during the first 48 hours of the flu (it is not effective after this time), and it should be used unless another remedy is obviously indicated.

☤ Gelsemium

When fatigue and a generalized heavy, weak feeling pervades the person, even leading to heavy, half-open eyelids, this remedy should be considered. People with these symptoms tend to have little or no thirst, can experience chills up and down their spine, and have a headache in the back part of their head.

☤ Bryonia

People who have marked body aches during their bout of flu that are aggravated by any type of motion suggest the need for this remedy. Generally, these people also have a headache in the front part of their head that is also aggravated by motion, have dry or chapped lips, a dry cough, and a great thirst for cold water.

☤ Eupatorium perfoliatum

People with the flu who experience aches in the muscles and who have pains in the bones often benefit from this remedy. Another characteristic symptom of people who need this remedy is that they may have chills that occur in the morning, especially between 7 and 9 A.M.

☤ Rhus toxicodendron

This remedy is effective for people with muscle aches that are aggravated by initial motion but relieved by continued motion. These people are often very restless, especially at night in bed, tend to have a sore throat, and are very thirsty but only for sips of water at a time.

☤ Influenzinum

If a person develops long-lasting symptoms after a bout of the flu, give a single dose of this remedy in the 30th or 200th potency.

INSOMNIA

Conventional drugs for insomnia tend to help a person fall asleep but ultimately lead them to wake up unrefreshed. To make things worse, these drugs tend to be addictive and tend to make falling asleep on one's own more difficult. Homeopathic medicines offer a safer alternative.

Use the 6th, 12th, or 30th potency every 30 minutes, up to three doses. Consider another remedy if sleep does not occur. If insomnia is a chronic problem, seek professional homeopathic care.

♟ Coffea
When a person feels overactive mentally and physically (these are the symptoms that coffee is well known to cause!), consider this remedy. However, it is also known to cause insomnia in people who are anticipating something exciting that will be occurring in the near future and in people who have a constant flow of ideas that keep them awake.

♟ Ignatia
People with insomnia who have suffered from a recent grieving experience often benefit from this remedy. Another characteristic symptom of people who need this remedy is that they tend to sigh or yawn frequently.

♟ Nux vomica
This remedy is indicated when insomnia results from consumption of alcohol, coffee, or drugs (therapeutic or recreational). This remedy is also useful for people with insomnia caused by mental strain or excessive study.

(Insomnia, cont'd.)

☒ Arsenicum

People with insomnia who suffer from various anxieties and fears often benefit from this remedy. Typically, such people are very anxious and restless, often causing them to get out of bed to walk around. They feel too tired and anxious to go to sleep.

☒ Gelsemium

People who feel anxiety about an upcoming event tend to benefit from this remedy. People with this type of anxiety tend to develop a dull and fatigued mind, making thinking an effort.

INFLAMMATORY BOWEL SYNDROME AND DISEASE

Inflammatory bowel syndrome refers to colitis, spastic colon, or simply nervous stomach, while inflammatory bowel disease refers to Crohn's disease and ulcerative colitis. Both of these ailments are chronic conditions that require the attention of a professional homeopath.

KNEE INJURIES

Knee injuries can be very painful, but what's worse is that they tend to recur in people who, for unknown reasons, cannot seem to heal their knee. Homeopathic remedies can help people truly heal a knee injury so that recurrence is less probable.

In addition to various remedies to be taken internally, there are also homeopathic external ones. One can also consider taking one of the homeopathic combination remedies both internally and externally. Generally, the sooner a homeopathic remedy is taken after the injury, the better the results.

Use the 6th or 30th potency every other hour during the first three doses and then four times a day after then until the healing is complete. It is generally recommended not to take the remedy for more than a week.

☒ **Ruta

This is the leading remedy for knee injuries. It is used for knee pain that is aggravated by any type of motion.

☒ Rhus toxicodendron

This remedy is indicated when the person feels pain upon initial motion but relief upon continued motion.

☒ Arnica

This remedy can be taken concurrently with the others above, and it is indicated when there is much swelling and bruising around the knee.

LEG CRAMPS

Leg cramps are a minor complaint that can be a real pain in the . . . leg. No one will die from leg cramps, but to those who experience them regularly, there is the feeling of being temporarily crippled. Some people benefit from the application of heat, some feel relief through massage or pressure, and some feel improvement after taking calcium tablets.

The correct homeopathic medicine often provides immediate relief. Take the 6th, 12th, or 30th potency every 30 minutes for up to three doses.

☒ **Cuprum metallicum

This is the leading homeopathic remedy for cramps in the calves and/or soles of the feet. The person may also feel some twitching or spasms in the leg muscle.

☒ Magnesium phosphorica

When a person with leg cramps feels relief from warm applications, consider this remedy.

M

Surrounded by
botanicals, they
are a part of us.

MASTITIS

Commonly experienced by nursing mothers, this complaint is quite painful due to the physical discomfort that it creates and because of the emotional dramas that it leads to, since a mother cannot easily breastfeed her infant.

Homeopathic medicines often provide rapid relief for women with mastitis. Use the 6th, 12th, or 30th potency every two hours during intense pain, and every four hours during more mild discomfort. If pain is not obviously reduced after three doses, consider another remedy.

☒ **Belladonna
This remedy is indicated when the breast is very red and inflamed and when the woman has a high fever, flushed face, and a throbbing headache. Women who need this remedy tend to have had a very rapid onset of symptoms.

☒ Bryonia
This remedy is another common remedy for mastitis and is valuable when the woman feels breast pain due to any type of motion, including deep breathing. The woman may even lie on their painful breast as a way to reduce its motion from breathing. The pain tends to be sharp and stitching. Women who need this remedy have usually had a slower onset of symptoms than those who need *Belladonna*.

☒ Phytolacca
For the second stage of mastitis when the breast becomes lumpy, stony hard, tender in spots, and pain radiates to the whole body, this is the remedy to consider. The woman may also have swollen lymph nodes in her armpit.

☒ Hepar sulphuris
Women who experience sharp, splinterlike pains in the breast, who emit a sour-smelling discharge from the breast, and who are extremely sensitive to cold air or cold application should consider this remedy.

Castor equi
Women with sore, deeply cracked nipples often benefit from this remedy. These women experience great sensitivity in the nipple area even when they're lightly touched or when they come in contact with clothing.

MEASLES

Recent research reported in a conventional medical journal showed that children who have had the measles have significantly fewer allergies than those given a measles vaccination. It might be immunologically useful for children to experience the infectious diseases of childhood.

Measles is usually a relatively mild disease, but it can be dangerous in malnourished children. In addition to giving homeopathic medicine, it is recommended to give vitamin A to children with the measles.

Use the 6th, 12th, or 30th potency every four hours during the first day and four times a day for up to two more days.

Aconitum
This remedy is indicated during the first stage of the measles when there is a sudden onset of fever, a skin rash, nasal discharge, reddened eyes, dry cough, and restless sleep.

Euphrasia
This remedy is recommended when, along with the skin rash, the predominant symptoms are a nasal discharge that does not irritate the nostrils and frequent tears from the eyes that burn and irritate the cheeks. The child may experience a dry cough, hoarseness, and a throbbing headache.

Gelsemium
When great fatigue and muscle aches are the leading symptoms, consider this remedy. Typically, the child feels very heavy and tired, physically and emotionally listless, and has little thirst.

Pulsatilla
This remedy is indicated after the beginning stages of measles are complete. Children may have a yellow or greenish nasal discharge and feel emotionally clingy

and weepy. They feel bad in stuffy or warm rooms and demand to have an open window and fresh air.

☒ Sulphur
When the skin rash is aggravated and becomes itchy by exposure to heat, by being in bed, and while taking a warm bath, this remedy should be considered. Typically, the children's eyelids are inflamed, and they feel burning in their eyes.

MENOPAUSE

Menopause itself is not a disease, although women commonly experience dis-easing symptoms during this change of life period. Hot flashes, vaginal dryness, osteoporosis, and various emotional changes are the most common symptoms.

Homeopathic medicines can help a woman through this change-of-life period and sharply reduce the physical discomforts and the emotional vicissitudes that are commonly experienced. Homeopaths have found that the best results are obtained from prescribing what are called "constitutional remedies"—that is, those based on the totality of physical and psychological symptoms that a woman is experiencing. As such, constitutional treatment requires the care of a professional homeopath.

MISCARRIAGES

Miscarriages are dramatic, traumatic, and sad events, but they are also a part of nature's efforts to let a woman give birth to only those beings that can reasonably sustain themselves. Treating a woman during pregnancy is a great way to strengthen her health so that she can complete her pregnancy in a healthy manner. There have not been any studies to verify homeopathy's ability to reduce miscarriage, but it is reasonable to assume that it does, since many women under homeopathic care feel that their health has improved. Women who wish to prevent a miscarriage should seek professional homeopathic care.

There are, however, some useful remedies that women can learn to use themselves if and when miscarriage takes place. These remedies will not necessarily prevent future miscarriages, but they will help the woman reestablish physical and emotional health after this dramatic and traumatic event.

Use the 6th, 12th, or 30th potency every hour for the first three doses, and then every four hours during the rest of the day and the day afterwards. Stop taking the remedy if there has already been a significant improvement.

☤ Arnica
This remedy is the leading one to help a woman get over the *physical* shock and trauma of a miscarriage.

☤ Ignatia
This remedy is the best one for helping a woman get over the *emotional* shock and trauma of a miscarriage. It is also the most important remedy for helping deal with the acute stages of grief from the loss of a loved one.

☤ Cinchona
Consider this remedy if the woman has lost a lot of blood and is now greatly fatigued.

MORNING SICKNESS

Recent research has suggested that women who experience morning sickness are less likely to miscarry. While this is certainly good news, the experience of morning sickness carries with it its own problems, including nausea that makes eating and nourishing oneself difficult. There is nothing that conventional medicine offers for this common ailment, but there is much evidence that homeopathic remedies aid women during this difficult time.

Use the 30th potency three times a day. If there is no improvement after the first 36 hours, consider another remedy. Stop taking the remedy when improvement begins, and restart only if symptoms return. Consider seeking professional homeopathic attention if symptoms are severe or if self-prescribed remedies aren't working well enough.

☒ **Sepia

This is one of the most common remedies for morning sickness. It is indicated when even the thought or smell of food causes nausea, or when there is an empty feeling in the stomach that is not relieved by eating. There is often a desire for pickles, vinegar, and sour foods. The woman can be irritable, depressed, and is usually averse to sex. Keeping busy and exercising provides some short-term relief.

☒ Colchicum

This is another common remedy for morning sickness. The sight or smell of food (especially eggs and fish) causes nausea, and symptoms are made worse by motion and turning the head. She may crave various foods but becomes averse to them upon smelling them. There is distention in the abdomen and burning or chilliness in that region as well. Women who need this remedy tend to be very weak and may even faint.

☒ Ipecacuahna

This remedy is for persistent nausea that is not at all relieved by vomiting. Despite the nausea, the woman's tongue is uncoated and clean. She may have a lot of saliva but little or no thirst.

☒ Nux vomica

Women who need this remedy have nausea, vomiting, and heartburn. They have a desire for coffee but get indigestion from it. They feel chilly and are aggravated by exposure to cold. They are highly irritable and become upset over the slightest thing.

☒ Tabacum

This remedy is indicated when women are cold, clammy, and pale while experiencing nausea. These individuals feel better in the open air, and the least motion can aggravate the nausea.

☒ Phosphorus

Women who develop a strong craving for ice drinks but then vomit them up once the water gets warm in their stomach often benefit from this remedy. It is also indicated for sociable women who are very sympathetic to the needs and pains of others.

112

homeopathy a-z

MOTION SICKNESS

Motion sickness is a relatively easy condition to treat using homeopathic remedies. You can either consider using one of the remedies listed below, or one of the homeopathic combination remedies for motion sickness that are available at most health food stores and at select pharmacies.

Use the 6th, 12th, or 30th potency every 30 minutes. If there is no improvement after 90 minutes, consider another remedy.

☒ **Cocculus

This is the most common remedy for motion sickness and should be given unless another remedy is obviously indicated. It helps reduce nausea, vomiting, headache, and dizziness associated with this condition.

☒ Tabacum

When those with motion sickness develop nausea and become cold, clammy, sweaty, and pale, consider this remedy. They may vomit and then feel tremulous weakness. It is particularly common for seasickness.

☒ Petroleum

People with motion sickness who develop a great emptiness and/or heartburn in the stomach that is relieved by eating suggest the need for this remedy. These people may also have a headache in the back of the head.

homeopathy a-z

MUMPS

Mumps is a common, usually not serious, childhood infectious disease that can cause complications if one gets the mumps after puberty. Whether it occurs in childhood or adulthood, homeopathic medicines can help the healing process.

Use the 6th, 12th, or 30th potency every four hours for up to three days. If improvement isn't noticed after one day, consider another remedy.

☷ Belladonna

This is a common remedy for the first stage of the mumps infection, especially when the illness begins suddenly and the child develops a reddened face and swollen and hot throat glands.

☷ Mercurius

This is a common remedy for the second stage of the mumps infection, especially when the child has a bad taste in the mouth, bad breath, and increased salivation. This child also tends to be sensitive to extremes of temperature and may sweat profusely.

☷ Pulsatilla

This remedy can be useful in second-stage mumps or in adult-onset cases, especially when the person is aggravated by stuffy or warm rooms, feels better in cool air, has little or no thirst, and has physical and emotional symptoms that constantly change.

☷ Phytolacca

This remedy is indicated when the salivary glands become very firm or hard and when there are shooting pains into the ear when swallowing.

Hold someone close to you and breathe with them

NAUSEA AND VOMITING

The nausea and vomiting reflexes are vital defenses of our body even though they don't always feel that way when we experience them. Homeopathic remedies can help a person heal from whatever is causing the nausea and vomiting.

Use the 6th, 12th, or 30th potency every two hours for the first three doses and, if necessary, every four hours after then for the next day. Consider changing remedies if there is no improvement after the three doses.

Ipecacuanha
This remedy is one of the most common for this condition. It is indicated when the person experiences constant nausea, which vomiting doesn't ameliorate. Despite the nausea, the person's tongue is clean and uncoated and there is little or no thirst. These people may also experience bleeding somewhere (that is, women may have a profuse menstruation; children or men may have a nosebleed).

Nux vomica
This is a leading remedy for nausea and/or vomiting that may be brought on by overconsumption of food or drink (alcohol), drugs (recreational or therapeutic), or mental stress from overwork. People who need this remedy tend to be very irritable and impatient.

Arsenicum
When the person has nausea and/or vomiting along with diarrhea, burning pains, weakness, and restlessness, this remedy is often indicated. These people have a great thirst but can only handle small sips at a time. This is the leading remedy for traveler's diarrhea along with nausea and vomiting.

Phosphorus
Consider this remedy when the person with nausea and/or vomiting has a great thirst for cold or ice drinks that make them feel better but tend to be vomited up once they become warm in the stomach.

(Nausea and Vomiting, cont'd.)

☒ Aethusa

People with nausea and/or vomiting as a result of intolerance to milk may benefit from this remedy. It is of particular value in treating infants.

☒ Bryonia

People who feel digestive discomfort after any type of motion may be helped by this remedy. These people tend to be constipated, irritable, want to be alone, and have a great thirst for cold liquids. Typically, these people have a feeling of pressure in their stomach, as though there was a stone there, and they feel nauseated and faint upon sitting up or standing.

☒ Lycopodium

This is a leading remedy for people with nausea who experience bloating, gas, and belching. People who need this medicine have an abdomen that is sensitive to any pressure, whether it is from a belt or elastic waistband. Typically, their symptoms worsen between 4 and 8 P.M. People who benefit from this remedy tend to crave sweets and tend to feel full after eating only a small amount of food, although this doesn't always stop them from eating.

NERVE INJURIES

Conventional medicine offers nothing for nerve injuries except painkillers and time. Homeopathic medicines offer some very effective remedies. Use the 6th or 30th potency every other hour for the first four doses, and then four times a day for up to four days.

☒ **Hypericum
This is the leading remedy for injuries to the nerves as evidenced by sharp and shooting pains.

☒ Magnesium phosphorica
If cramping is concurrent with nerve injury, consider this remedy.

☒ Coffea
If *Hypericum* does not work well enough, consider this remedy.

OVARIAN CYSTS OR TUMORS

Ovarian cysts or tumors represent systemic chronic problems that require the care of a professional homeopath.

OVEREXERTION

It is often good to push yourself physically; the problem is when you overexert yourself. Muscle fatigue and muscle aches are the common result of such exertion. There are, however, simple remedies to prevent and reduce the trauma of overexertion.

If you know that you will be overexerting yourself, take *Arnica* and/or *Lacticum acidum* in the 30th potency just prior to the activity. If the activity lasts over one hour, take another dose every hour. Use the 30th potency every hour after the exertion for three doses, and if pain is still felt, take it every other hour for the next 24 hours.

(Overexertion, cont'd.)

☒ **Arnica

This is the leading remedy to prevent and reduce the effects of overexertion.

☒ Rhus toxicodendron

If the person becomes stiff and achy from overexertion and feels increased pain upon initial motion, consider this remedy.

☒ Lacticum acidum

Made from lactic acid, this remedy is thought to help the body reabsorb lactic acid, a by-product from muscle tissue as the result of exertion, and thereby, it can often reduce fatigue from exertion.

POISON IVY, OAK, OR SUMAC

The rash from poison ivy, oak, or sumac is called contact dermatitis, and it can be extremely irritating. Conventional medicines for such rashes are usually corticosteroids; however, due to the powerful immunosuppressive effects, it is recommended to use these drugs only when the rash is particularly disturbing and if homeopathic medicines aren't working well.

Use the 6th, 12th, or 30th potency every other hour in intense cases, and four times a day during mild symptoms. If improvement is not noticeable after 24 hours, consider another remedy. It is rarely necessary to take a remedy for longer than four days.

☒ **Anacardium

This is one of the most common remedies for this condition. It is particularly indicated when there is much swelling along with the rash, and the person's symptoms feel better in a bath of very hot water.

☒ Rhus toxicodendron

While some of the other remedies listed here are not always available at the local health food store, this remedy is usually there and is often effective for this condition. It is particularly indicated when the person's symptoms are worse at night in bed, the person becomes extremely restless, the person desires milk or milk products, and scratching aggravates the itching.

☒ Croton tiglium

The key symptom of people who need this remedy is that their skin feels hidebound or tight all over. Another characteristic symptom is that they feel better after sleep.

☒ Graphites

If a person's rash develops pustules that exude a glutinous, honeylike discharge, consider this remedy.

☒ Sulphur

This remedy should be considered when the person's symptoms are aggravated by warmth of any kind, when scratching causes itching and burning pains, and the person maintains a generally unkempt appearance.

PREGNANCY

Pregnancy is a great time to take homeopathic remedies because they offer benefit to both mother and fetus. Also, because conventional drugs are generally thought to be potentially dangerous to the fetus, homeopathic remedies offer a considerably safer alternative. Although there have not been any formal studies that have recorded possible side effects of homeopathic remedies during pregnancy, 200 years of experience by homeopathic physicians suggests a high level of safety with these natural remedies.

There are numerous types of complaints that women have during pregnancy, and it is impossible to list them all in a book such as this. Readers are encouraged to look up specific symptoms in this or other homeopathic guidebooks and are particularly encouraged to seek out such guidebooks for pregnant women (there are several books of this type are available).

There are no single homeopathic remedies that will benefit all pregnant women because they require more individualization of the woman's specific symptoms.

PREMENSTRUAL CRAMPS

Too many women live with the pain of menstruation, not knowing that there are some simple and safe ways to reduce their discomfort. Homeopathic remedies provide a safe and effective treatment for most women's menstrual cramps.

Although professional homeopathic care can help reduce the chronically recurrence menstrual problems, women can often effectively treat themselves for acute menstrual cramps with the remedies listed below.

Use the 6th, 12th, or 30th potency every 30 minutes during intense cramps for the first three doses, and use them every four hours during less intense cramps. If pain is not reduced after three to five doses, consider taking another remedy.

☖ Belladonna
Cramps with throbbing pains that come on suddenly, go away suddenly, and then return suddenly commonly suggest this remedy. These pains tend to be worse on the right side, although they don't have to

be there in every instance. Motion aggravates the pain, and there is some relief when sitting in a semierect position. When the menstruation begins, it is profuse, bright red, and gushing.

⚱ Magnesia phosphorica
Cramps that are relieved by bending forward or by applying warm applications suggest the need for this remedy.

⚱ Colocynthis
Cramps that are relieved by applying strong pressure indicate this remedy. Consider using it when women feel some reduction in pain by bending over a chair that applies strong pressure to their painful abdomen. Typically, the woman is also very irritable.

⚱ Cimicifuga
This remedy is useful when a woman experiences sharp cramps that seem to dart from one side to another and that cause such pain that she blurt out loud that she can't take it anymore.

⚱ Pulsatilla
Women who get weepy and moody during their premenstrual cramps and who want sympathy and affection during this time suggest the need for this remedy. Women who experience varying and changing symptoms strongly indicate this remedy as well.

☒ Lachesis

This remedy is useful for irritable, angry, and jealous women with menstrual cramps who cannot stand any tight clothing, especially around the neck. Typically, this remedy is good for women with cramps that are primarily on the left side and that are worse in the morning upon waking up.

PUNCTURE WOUNDS

Deep puncture wounds, puncture wounds from rusty nails, and those from previously used needles require medical attention, but the average puncture wound can be treated at home with simple hygiene and homeopathic remedies.

In addition to the homeopathic remedies listed below that are taken internally, one might consider applying *Hypericum* tincture or spray externally on deep wounds; and *Calendula* tincture, ointment, gel, or spray externally on superficial wounds. Reapply after every washing or at least once a day.

Use the 6th, 12th, or 30th potency three times a day for up to two days.

☒ **Ledum

This is the leading remedy for puncture wounds.

☒ Hypericum

If there are shooting pains from the puncture wound, consider this remedy.

☒ Apis

Use this remedy if the puncture wound feels warm or hot, is aggravated by application of heat, and is relieved by application of cold.

☒ Staphysagria

This remedy is indicated for stab wounds from a knife, especially to the abdomen.

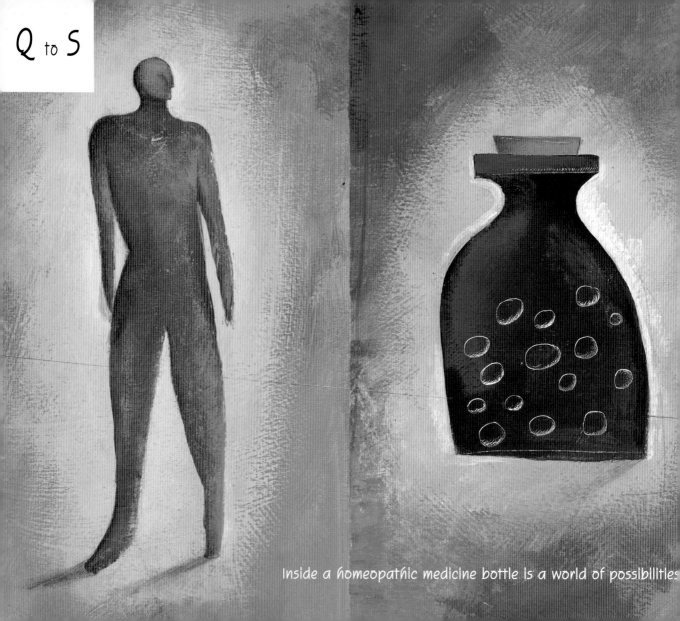

Inside a homeopathic medicine bottle is a world of possibilities

SHOCK OF INJURY

First-aid courses commonly teach people that it is most important to treat seriously injured people for shock of injury first, except when there is serious bleeding that needs immediate attention. The state of shock slows down circulation of blood and oxygen to the head and brain and can lead to the death of brain cells. A person who remains in a state of shock too long can have lifelong complications from it. Shock, with the exception of mild cases, is a medical emergency.

People in shock often do not know it because a part of their condition is that the inadequate levels of oxygen to their brain causes them to think less than clearly. When people experience an injury and their face is pale or grayish, they should be treated for shock: Lay the person down with their feet elevated, keep them from getting too cold or too warm, stop any blood loss with direct pressure, and make certain that their airways are clear.

One other good piece of advice in treating a person for shock is to give a homeopathic remedy, which can have rapid and beneficial effects on someone in shock. Give the remedy as *soon* as possible after the injury. Use the 30th potency every 30 minutes until the person is clearly out of shock. If there is no obvious improvement after two doses, consider another remedy and seek professional medical care.

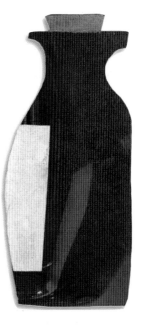

homeopathy a–z

♁ **Arnica

This is the most common remedy for shock of injury; unless some other remedy is clearly indicated, *Arnica* should be given. It is useful for both mild and serious levels of shock.

♁ Aconitum

This remedy is indicated for shock of injury when the person is full of anxiety or fear, usually relating to death or impending doom.

♁ Carbo vegetabilis

If the person in shock is weak and collapsed, wants to be fanned, and has a pale-bluish skin color, consider this remedy.

SINUSITIS

Sinusitis is a very common ailment that can result from a bacterial, viral, or fungal infection, as well as from an allergy. It can have mild or intense symptoms.

Homeopathic remedies can be effectively used to keep the pain and discomfort from sinusitis to a minimum.

Use the 6th, 12th, or 30th potency every four hours during intense symptoms, and three times a day during more mild symptoms. If there is no improvement after 24 hours, consider another remedy.

♁ **Kali bichromicum

This is the most common remedy for sinus problems, especially when there is pain at the very root of the nose and/or the person has a thick, stringy nasal discharge. Typically, the pain begins in the morning, worsens until noon, and lessens by the late afternoon.

☧ Pulsatilla

This is a common remedy for women and children (although it can also be given to men) when the person's symptoms are worse at night, in warm rooms, lying down or stooping; and when the pains are reduced when the person is outside in the open air, in the morning, and with pressure on the painful areas. Typically, the person prefers the company of others, desires attention and sympathy during painful times, and may cry from the pain and discomfort.

☧ Hepar sulphurls

This remedy is indicated when the person is aggravated by exposure to cold air, and is hypersensitive to touch and to movement of the head.

☧ Mercurlus

Consider this remedy when the person develops bad breath and strong body odor, is sensitive to extremes of temperature, and the symptoms are worse near drafts and at night.

SORE THROAT

Symptoms of sore throat may result from a bacterial or viral infection or from irritation as the result of a cough. Most sore throats are self-limiting and can and will eventually heal by themselves, but homeopathic remedies can reduce the pain and discomfort and speed up a person's healing.

Many people are fearful of developing a strep throat, not because the infection itself is a problem, but because it is thought that the infection can spread to the heart and cause a serious condition called rheumatic fever. What is not commonly recognized today is that rheumatic fever has almost disappeared—even for people who have strep throat and don't take antibiotics. Furthermore, when rheumatic fever has occurred in the recent past, the vast majority of cases included people who didn't even have a sore throat within the previous three months, and for those people who did have a sore throat, the vast majority of them took antibiotics and still got rheumatic fever. This research suggests that rheumatic fever today is not related to strep throat or simple sore throats, and antibiotics are not effective in preventing rheumatic fever when one does have strep throat.

Homeopathic remedies offer a more reasonable alternative to antibiotics, especially since many sore throats are viral. Use the 6th, 12th, or 30th potency every four hours for the first three doses and then, if necessary, four times a day for not longer than two days. If symptoms do not improve after about the first three doses, consider another remedy.

☒ Aconitum

Consider using this remedy during the first 24 hours, especially if there is rapid onset from exposure to cold weather and the person has a noticeably increased thirst.

☒ Belladonna

This remedy is generally useful during the first 48 hours and is particularly effective when the person has reddened tonsils, burning pain in the throat, flushed red skin, and a fever. The tonsils may be swollen but there will be no pus on them.

☒ Apis

This medicine is valuable when the person has noticeably red and swollen tonsils and a burning, stinging throat pain that is relieved by sucking on ice or cold things and aggravated by eating or drinking warm things.

☒ Hepar sulphuris

In the later stages of a sore throat when pus has developed, this remedy is often useful, especially when there is a sensation of a splinter or something stuck in the throat, when the throat is sensitive to any touch or swallowing, and when the person is irritated by exposure to cold of any kind.

☒ Lachesis

When a person develops a sore throat that is noticeably worse on the left side and that begins on the left and moves to the right, consider this remedy. People who benefit from it also tend to be sensitive to any clothing around the neck, tend to have an aggravation of symptoms upon waking in the morning, and tend to feel worse in general from exposure to heat.

☒ Lycopodium

This remedy should be considered for people who experience a sore throat on the right side, or one that starts on the right and moves to the left. Another characteristic symptom of people who need this remedy is that they are relieved by warm drinks or warm food and feel worse between 4 and 8 P.M.

☒ Phytolacca

This remedy is important in the later stages of a sore throat, especially when the throat is dark red or perhaps bluish or purplish, the person has repeated desires to swallow, there are swollen neck glands and a sensation of a lump in the throat, and the throat pain sometimes extends to the ear upon swallowing. These people feel worse when swallowing warm or hot drinks and may be unable to do so.

SPRAINS AND STRAINS

Sports medicine doctors recommend the "RICE" treatment (rest, ice, compression, and elevation) to treat sprains and strains, and at best, conventional physicians add painkillers to this treatment plan. People should know that painkillers do not get rid of the pain; they simply block a person's consciousness about the pain they are experiencing. The problem here is that injured people who take painkillers tend to use their injured part because they aren't conscious of the pain, and then further aggravate the injury. Whether a person uses their injured part or not, research has shown that painkillers actually slow down the healing of injuries.

Homeopathic remedies offer a safe and often effective means to speed up the healing of a sprain or strain. In fact, a lot of people get introduced to homeopathy through self-treating for this common injury.

People with sprains and strains benefit from taking homeopathic internal and external remedies concurrently. External remedies should be applied at least twice a day. It may also make sense to use homeopathic combination remedies internally and externally for sprains and strains. These products have several remedies in them for the various types of tissue trauma that is experienced.

Please note that it may be necessary to take *Arnica* for the first two to four doses to reduce the shock of injury and to keep the injured part from swelling too much. After then, it may be necessary to take another remedy to heal the sprain or strain.

Try to take a homeopathic remedy as *soon* after injury as possible. People who take the remedy immediately are often surprised to find out that there is no or little sign of the injury by the next day. Give *Arnica* in the 6th, 12th, or 30th potency every hour for the first three doses. Then, give another indicated remedy after this every other hour for three to six doses, depending upon the severity, and then every fourth hour as the pain decreases.

☒ **Arnica

Take this remedy immediately after the injury. It will help reduce the pain, swelling, and bruising.

☒ **Rhus toxicodendron

This is the leading remedy for the sprain or strain itself, especially when the pain is worse upon initial motion and is not as severe as the person continues to move. Then, after the person rests again, the injured part gets stiff and is aggravated by initial motion.

☒ Ruta

This remedy is for severe sprains, when a person has wrenched a tendon or torn a ligament. It is also indicated for injuries to the knee or elbow.

☒ Bryonia

Consider this remedy if any type of motion aggravates the injured part.

☒ Ledum

This remedy is useful for ankle sprains, especially when the injured area feels cold and feels relieved by cold applications.

☒ Strontium carbonicum

People who develop chronic sprains tend to benefit from this remedy. Some people may, however, need professional homeo-pathic care for a constitutional remedy.

STOMACHACHE

Stomach or abdominal pain can be a minor ailment as a result of indigestion, gas, menstrual cramps, or emotional stress, or it can represent a serious illness (liver problems, inflammation of the gall bladder or pancreas, intestinal disease or obstruction, cancer, ectopic pregnancy, or miscarriage). Consult medical guidebooks or a physician to determine if your complaint is serious or not, and in the meantime, consider using homeopathic remedies to provide some relief.

Use the 6th, 12th, or 30th potency every hour or every other hour during intense pain, and every four to six hours when there is more mild pain. If there is no improvement after three doses, consider another remedy.

☿ Pulsatilla

Commonly given to children and women, this remedy is known for stomach pain or heartburn after the ingestion of fatty foods (ice cream, fried food) or pork, when there is a lack of thirst, an aversion to stuffy rooms, and a desire for open air. Typically, these people are highly emotional and desire sympathy and attention.

☿ Bryonia

People who feel digestive discomfort after any type of motion may be helped by this remedy. People who need it tend to be constipated, irritable, want to be alone, and have a great thirst for cold liquids. Stomach pains after eating, and constipation with much dryness of the stools also suggest this remedy.

☒ Cuprum metallicum

Strong cramping pains in the abdomen that are aggravated by motion or by touching and that may be accompanied by vomiting are characteristic of those who need this remedy.

☒ Magnesia phosphorica

Strong cramping pains that are relieved by warm applications or by bending over suggest the need for this remedy.

☒ Lycopodium

This is a leading remedy for people who experience bloating, gas, and belching. People who need it have an abdomen that is sensitive to any pressure, whether it is from a belt or elastic waistband. Typically, their symptoms are worse between 4 and 8 P.M.

☒ Arsenicum

This is a leading remedy for indigestion when people have burning pains, a great thirst but for only sips at a time, feelings of chilliness, a general restlessness, and anxiety about one's health. These people experience an aggravation of their symptoms at midnight and afterwards.

☒ Nux vomica

Stomach pain that starts after overeating; after overconsumption of alcohol, coffee, or drugs (therapeutic or recreational); or after mental stress is commonly relieved by this remedy. Heartburn, nausea, and gas are usually accompanied by increased irritability.

☒ Sulphur

People with heartburn from overeating or eating the wrong foods and who may also suffer from early-morning diarrhea often benefit from this remedy. Typically, these people tend to feel a generalized heat from their body that makes exposure to cool or cold air feel good and leads to an aggravation of symptoms from warmth or heat.

STYES

A stye is a minor condition, and complications from it are rare, but it is still irritating and its discomfort can be relieved with homeopathic remedies.

Use the 6th, 12th, or 30th potency every four to six hours. It isn't necessary to give a remedy longer than 24 hours.

☒ Pulsatilla
This remedy is useful for relatively painless styes usually on the upper lid. In later stages, a yellow or greenish discharge may occur.

☒ Hepar sulphuris
When a stye is painful and hypersensitive to touch or cold, consider this remedy. A characteristic symptom is if it feels as though a splinter is in the person's eye.

☒ Apis
A stye with a lot of swelling of the lid and with burning and/or stinging pains that are aggravated by heat and relieved by cold suggests this remedy.

SUNSTROKE OR HEATSTROKE

Sunstroke can be a life-threatening emergency. Homeopathic remedies can be helpful, but they should be given while the person is being taken to a doctor.

Use the 6th, 12th, or 30th potency every 30 minutes for the first two hours. If there is no obvious improvement, consider another remedy. After giving a remedy for two hours, reduce the frequency to every one to four hours, depending upon the intensity of the person's symptoms.

☒ Belladonna

This is the leading remedy for people with a fever, throbbing headache, reddened face, dilated pupils, and stupor. This remedy is in every homeopathic medicine kit, while *Glonoine* isn't. Because treatment must begin as soon as possible, give *Belladonna* unless you have *Glonoine* and you are confident that *Glonoine* is the correct remedy.

☒ Glonoine

This remedy is for those with symptoms similar to those mentioned above, although these people tend to feel worse when they bend their head backward and when cold water is applied to them, which can cause spasms.

SURGERY

Professional homeopaths can often prescribe homeopathic remedies that can prevent the need for surgery, but sometimes the best and only appropriate treatment for a person is a surgical procedure. It is good to know that homeopathic remedies can complement surgery and help a person recover more quickly.

It is best to individualize a homeopathic remedy based on the symptoms that individuals are experiencing. For instance, if they are having indigestion or a headache after surgery, rather than use one of the remedies below, look in the Indigestion or Headache sections of this book.

Use the 30th potency of *Arnica* just prior to the surgery and immediately afterwards in order to help with the surgical shock. Thirty minutes after taking the second dose of *Arnica*, use the 6th or 30th potency of *Arnica* or the indicated remedy every other hour during the first day, and every four to six hours during the second day. Consider taking a remedy until the pain is minimal or gone, usually not longer than four days.

☱ Arnica

If there is much bruising and black and blueness under the skin, take this remedy. Also, use it to relieve the pain of bedsores.

☱ Aconitum

If a person experiences great fear or anxiety after the surgery and even thinks he or she is dying, consider this remedy immediately.

☱ Hypericum

If surgery included nerve-rich areas, such as the head, back, eyes, toes, and hands; or if there are any sharp or shooting pains, use this remedy. This is also an important remedy for amputations and for dental surgery.

☱ Staphysagria

For abdominal surgery, caesarian section, episiotomy, circumcision, or prostate surgery, consider this remedy.

☱ Ruta

Any dental or bone surgery should include use of this remedy.

☱ Bellis perennis

For breast surgery, whether it is for cosmetic or therapeutic reasons, consider this remedy.

☱ Calendula (external application)

Use this remedy externally on the surgical incision in order to speed its healing.

☱ Hypericum (external application)

Use this remedy externally on deep surgical incisions in order to speed healing.

Homeopathic medicines radiate their fields of force.

TEETHING

Teething is a problem that drives infants and their parents crazy, yet it is a simple problem that homeopathic remedies take care of easily. In addition to the single remedies listed below, there are homeopathic combination remedies that are readily accessible at health food stores and pharmacies that are wonderfully effective.

If you can't figure out which single remedy to use, it is simple to just get homeopathic teething tablets. Homeopathic remedies act very rapidly on teething infants. Usually one dose per episode is all that is needed, although sometimes a second dose is necessary. Use the 6th, 12th, or 30th potency.

☒ **Chamomilla

This is the most common remedy for teething. It is indicated for infants who are very irritable, who demand something but push it away when it is offered, and who only stop crying temporarily while they are held and rocked and then start up again when they are placed down. This is also a common remedy for infants with diarrhea or an earache along with teething.

☒ Calcarea carbonica

This remedy is useful in infants who begin teething a tad late, and usually in babies with a lot of baby fat who sweat profusely, especially on the head.

☒ Belladonna

Consider this remedy when the baby's gums are noticeably red, swollen, and throbbing. Typically, such babies have a flushed, red face and glassy eyes, with much heat emanating from the body but little or no sweat.

☒ Calcarea phosphorica

This remedy is indicated in infants who are peevish, fretful, and discontented. The baby wants to nurse often but is frequently gaseous. Such babies tend to be pale and thin.

☒ Silicea

Infants who are frail, delicate, and constipated often benefit from this remedy.

TENDINITIS
(see Sprains and Strains)

THROAT
(see Sore Throat)

TOOTHACHE

God bless whatever works to help relieve the pain of a toothache. Such pain can be excruciating, and it is good to know that homeopathic remedies provide one option for people.

Use the 6th, 12th, or 30th potencies every 30 minutes during intense pain, and every two to four hours during more mild pain. If there is no improvement after three doses, consider another remedy.

☒ Hepar sulphuris
This is a common remedy for sharp, needlelike pains from abscessed teeth, especially when the tooth is extremely sensitive to touch and to cold things. Bad breath is typically also present.

☒ Coffea
When a toothache is temporarily relieved by holding cold water in the mouth but gets worse as the water gets warm, consider this remedy. Typically, the toothache drives the person to be extremely physically and mentally restless.

☒ Ruta

This is a leading remedy for people who experience pain after dental surgery. It is also an important remedy for dry socket.

☒ Belladonna

People with a throbbing toothache that comes and goes and returns suddenly often benefit from this remedy. Usually those who need this remedy have gums that are extremely red, the mouth is dry, and the person's face may be flushed red.

☒ Chamomilla

People who experience violent toothaches, who get some relief by having cold water in the mouth, and are aggravated by warm food or drink tend to benefit from this remedy.

☒ Mercurius

People with severe tooth pain who salivate excessively suggest the need for this remedy. The tooth pain tends to be worse at night, from eating or drinking anything too hot or too cold, and the person may even have pain that extends to their ears or face. These people tend to have bad breath.

ULCERATIVE COLITIS
(see Inflammatory Bowel Syndrome and Disease)

ULCERS

Ulcers represent a serious enough disease that people should seek professional homeopathic care for their treatment.

VAGINITIS
(acute)

Vaginitis is an all-too-common complaint of women today. When women take antibiotics for infection in another part of their body, these drugs disturb the delicate microbial balance that exists in a woman's vagina, which can then lead to a vaginal infection. A woman can also get vaginitis from chemical irritation after exposure to diaphragm jellies, feminine hygiene products, tampons, or foreign objects in the vagina.

Because vaginitis could be the result of various possible infections, it is recommended to seek medical attention for an accurate diagnosis. Homeopathic remedies can be given before one goes to the doctor, along with whatever conventional medication is prescribed.

Women who experience repeated vaginitis should seek professional homeopathic care for constitutional treatment. Use the 6th, 12th, or 30th potency two to four times a day, depending upon the intensity of symptoms. Improvement

should occur within 24 hours. If there hasn't been any improvement during the first 24 hours, consider another remedy.

♟ Kreosotum

When the woman experiences great irritation, itching, rawness, and especially burning of the vagina with an offensive-smelling discharge that is irritating to the skin, consider this remedy. The vaginal discharge tends to be worse in the morning and upon standing.

♟ Borax

Vaginal discharges that are milky-white suggest the need for this remedy, especially when the woman has a strong sensitivity to sudden noise, a discharge that is worse midway between the menstrual cycle, and/or a discomfort from downward motions.

♀ Pulsatilla

This remedy is indicated in women who tend to be very weepy, moody, desirous of sympathy, averse to heat and warm rooms, crave open air, and are without thirst. The vaginal discharge could be of any color (the color and its attendant symptoms tend to be changeable) but is not usually of a burning nature.

♀ Sepia

Women with vaginitis who have a sensation of pressure or a weight that gives them a feeling of bearing-down pain suggest the need for this remedy. The woman is fatigued, depressed, irritable, and overwhelmed. Walking may aggravate symptoms, but vigorous exercise tends to invigorate the woman. This remedy is commonly used during and after pregnancy.

♀ Calcarea carbonica

This remedy tends to be indicated in women who are overweight, have loose muscle tone, are very chilly, and are easily exhausted.

WARTS

Warts are an extremely common skin problem that is usually easily and effectively treated with homeopathic remedies. If self-treatment is unsuccessful or if warts continue to return, professional homeopathic care is recommended because warts can be an expression of an underlying chronic malady.

One of the most common homeopathic medicines for warts is *Thuja*, and it is prescribed in internal and external applications (in ointment form). An external application should be applied at least once a day or after every washing. If improvement isn't obvious after 14 days, consider another remedy or seek professional homeopathic care. Use the 6th, 12th, or 30th potency of the indicated internal remedy twice a day for up to three days. Wait at least two weeks after the final dose to determine to the remedy has been successful. If not, consider another internal remedy. It is okay to use internal and external remedies concurrently.

(Warts, cont'd.)

☒ **Thuja

This is the most common homeopathic remedy for various kinds of warts, except plantar warts. If no other remedy is obviously indicated, consider this one. It is particularly indicated in isolated, jagged warts that may bleed and may smell foul. It is also common for warts on the genitals.

☒ Causticum

People who have old, large warts on the face (especially the nose) or on the tips of their fingers that bleed easily suggest the need for this remedy. The warts also tend to be hard, inflamed, and painful. People who benefit from this remedy tend to be intensely sympathetic to the pains and plights of others and tend to have a fear that something awful is impending.

☒ Nitric acid

This remedy is indicated in treating large, jagged warts that bleed upon washing them and that itch and sting. This remedy is also indicated in people who are in great anxiety about their health and who have a particular fear of cancer.

☒ Antimonium crudum

People who have hard, smooth warts; have a thickly coated white tongue; and who are excessively irritable suggest the need for this remedy. These people tend of overeat frequently and have various digestive complaints.

☒ Ruta

This is a leading remedy for plantar warts, especially on the palms of the hand.

A List of Remedies and Their Common Names

Aconitum: monkshood
Aesculus: horse chestnut
Aethusa: fly agaric
Allium cepa: onion
Aloe socotrina: socotrine aloes
Ambrosia: ragweed
Anacardium: marking nut
Antimonium crudum: black sulphide of antimony
Antimonium tarticum: tartar emetic
Apis: crushed bee
Argentum nitricum: nitrate of silver
Arnica: leopard's bane
Arsenicum: arsenic trioxide
Belladonna: deadly nightshade
Bellis perennis: daisy
Borax: biborate of sodium
Bryonia: white bryony
Calcarea carbonica: carbonate of lime
Calcarea phosphorica: phosphate of lime
Calendula: marigolds
Candida albicans: candida albicans (a yeast)
Cantharis: Spanish fly
Carbo vegetabilis: vegetable charcoal

Castor equi: rudimentary thumbnail of the horse
Caulophyllum: blue cohosh
Causticum: Hahnemann's *tinctura acris sine Kali*
Chamomilla: chamomile
Chelidonium: greater celandine
Cicuta: water hemlock
Cimicifuga: black snakeroot
Cina: wormseed
Cinchona: peruvian bark
Cocculus: Indian cockle
Coccus cacti: cochineal insect
Coffea: coffee
Colchicum: meadow saffron
Collinsonia: stone root
Colocynthus: bittle apple
Croton tiglium: croton oil seed
Cuprum metallicum: copper
Eupatorium perfoliatum: boneset
Euphrasia: eyebright
Gelsemium: yellow jessamine
Glonoine: nitroglycerine
Graphites: graphite
Hamamelis: witch hazel

Hellaborus: Christmas rose
Hepar sulphuris: Hahnemann's calcium
   sulphide
Histiminium: histimine
House dust mite: house dust mite
Hypericum: St. John's wort
Hyoscyamus: henbane
Ignatia: St. Ignatius bean
Influenzinum: influenza virus
Ipecacuahna: ipecac root
Iris: blue flag
Kali bichromicum: bichromate
   of potash
Kreosotum: beechwood kreosote
Lachesis: venom from the
   bushmaster
Lacticum acidum: lactic acid
Ledum: marsh tea
Lycopodium: club moss
Magnesium phosphorica: phosphate
   of magnesia
Mercurius: mercury
Natrum muriaticum: salt
Natrum sulphur: sulphate of sodium
Nitric acid: nitric acid
Nux vomica: poison nut

Oscillococcinum: heart and liver of a duck
Phosphorus: phosphorus
Phytolacca: pokeroot
Podophyllum: mayapple
Pulsatilla: windflower
Rhus toxicodendron: poison ivy
Rumex: yellow dock
Ruta: rue
Sabadilla: cevadilla seed
Sanguinaria: bloodroot
Sarsaparilla: smilax
Sepia: inky juice from the cuttlefish
Silicea: silica
Solidago: goldenrod
Spigelia: demerate pinkroot
Spongia: roasted sponge
Staphysagria: stavesacre
Stramonium: datura stramonium
Strontium carbonicum: carbonate of
   strontium
Sulphur: sulfur
Symphytum: comfrey
Tabacum: tobacco
Tarentula hispanica: Lycosa tarentula
Urtica urens: stinging nettle
Veratrum album: white hellebore

homeopathy a - z

APPENDIX

Inside each of us is the world outside of us.

HOMEOPATHIC ORGANIZATIONS

American Institute of Homeopathy
1585 Glencoe St. #44
Denver, CO 80220 ▪ (303) 321-4105

Founded in 1844 and the oldest national medical society in the United States, this organization admits only medical doctors and osteopaths as voting members. It publishes a journal and sponsors or co-sponsors an annual conference. It also interfaces with government agencies on issues relating to the homeopathic profession.

Council for Homeopathic Certification
1199 Sanchez St.
San Francisco, CA 94114 ▪ (415) 789-7677

This organization provides certification for licensed health professionals (M.D., D.O., N.D., D.C., P.A., R.N., C.A., D.D.S., etc.). A rigorous examination must be passed, as well as an analysis of at least ten cases.

Foundation for Homeopathic Education and Research
2124 Kittredge St.
Berkeley, CA 94704 ▪ (510) 649-8930

This organization works to educate the medical community and the general public about research in homeopathy. It provides speakers on homeopathic research to hospitals, medical schools, industry, and community groups.

Homeopathic Academy of Naturopathic Physicians
P.O. Box 12488
Portland, OR 97212 ▪ (503) 795-0579

This is the organization of naturopathic physicians who specialize in homeopathy. It certifies qualified naturopaths and publishes a professional journal.

National Center for Homeopathy
801 N. Fairfax, #306
Alexandria, VA 22314 ▪ (703) 548-7790

This is the most important homeopathic organization in the United States. They publish a monthly magazine, maintain an active network of homeopathic study groups, hold annual conferences and short summer training programs for laypeople and health professionals, and provide spokespersons to the media.

North American Society of Homeopaths (NASH)
2024 S. Deerborn St.
Seattle, WA 98144 ▪ (206) 720-7000

NASH certifies only unlicensed practitioners of homeopathy. To obtain certification, one must have completed an approved training program and clinical internship and pass a comprehensive examination in homeopathy. Although this certification does not grant legal right to practice homeopathy, it is beginning to lay the groundwork for a distinct profession of homeopaths.

homeopathy a t z

SOURCES OF HOMEOPATHIC REMEDIES

The following companies either manufacture homeopathic remedies or provide a mail-order service for them. Homeopathic remedies are also commonly available at health food stores and pharmacies, though the following companies provide a more extensive assortment of remedies, as well as homeopathic home medicine kits.

Biological Homeopathic Industries
11600 Cochiti S.E.
Albuquerque, NM 87123 ▪ (505) 293-3843

Boericke and Tafel
2381 Circadian Way
Santa Rosa, CA 95407 ▪ (707) 571-8202

Boiron, Inc.
6 Campus Blvd., Building A
Newtown Square, PA 19073 ▪ (610) 325-7464
also: 98c W. Cochran
Simi Valley, CA 93065 ▪ (805) 582-9091

Dolisos
3014 Rigel Rd.
Las Vegas, NV 89102 ▪ (702) 871-7153

Hahnemann Pharmacy
1940 4th St.
San Rafael, CA 94901 ▪ (415) 451-6970

Homeopathic Educational Services
2124 Kittredge St.
Berkeley, CA 94704 ▪ (510) 649-0294

Luyties Pharmacal
4200 Laclede Ave.
St. Louis, MO 63108 ▪ (314) 533-9600

Natra-Bio
1441 W. Smith Rd.
Bellingham, WA 98226 ▪ (206) 384-5656

Standard Homeopathic Company
204-210 W. 131st St.
Los Angeles, CA 90061 ▪ (310) 321-4284

Washington Homeopathic Pharmacy
4914 Del Ray Ave.
Bethesda, MD 20814 ▪ (301) 656-1695

HOMEOPATHIC BOOKS

*Particularly good books

Introductory and Family Guidebooks

Miranda Castro, *The Complete Homeopathy Handbook*. New York: St. Martin's, 1990.

*Stephen Cummings, M.D., and Dana Ullman, M.P.H., *Everybody's Guide to Homeopathic Medicine*. New York: Jeremy Tarcher/Putnam, 1997.

*Richard Grossinger, Ph.D.., *Homeopathy: The Great Riddle*. Berkeley: North Atlantic, 1998.

*Wayne Jonas, M.D., and Jennifer Jacobs, M.D., *Healing with Homeopathy*. New York: Warner, 1996.

*Thomas Kruzel, N.D., *Homeopathic Emergency Guide*. Berkeley: North Atlantic, 1992.

Andrew Lockie, M.D., *The Family Guide to Homeopathy*. New York: Fireside, 1993.

———, and Nicola Geddes, M.D., *The Complete Guide to Homeopathy*. New York: Dorling and Kindserly, 1995.

Maesimund Panos, M.D., and Jane Heimlich, *Homeopathic Medicine at Home*. New York: Jeremy Tarcher, 1980.

*Dana Ullman, M.P.H., *Discovering Homeopathy*. Berkeley: North Atlantic, 1991.

*———, *The Consumer's Guide to Homeopathy*. New York: Jeremy Tarcher/Putnam, 1996.

*Robert Ullman, N.D., and Judyth Reichenberg-Ullman, N.D., M.S.W., *The Quick and Simple Guide to Homeopathic Self-Care*. Rocklin, CA: Prima, 1997.

George Vithoulkas, *Homeopathy: Medicine for the New Man*. New York: Arco, 1979.

*Edward C. Whitmont, M.D., *The Alchemy of Healing*. Berkeley: North Atlantic, 1993.

Specialized Self-Care Books

*Miranda Castro, *Homeopathy for Pregnancy, Birth and Your Baby's First Year*. New York: St. Martin's, 1993.

*———, *Homeopathic Guide to Stress*. New York: St. Martin's, 1997.

Peter Chappel, *Emotional Healing with Homeopathy*. Rockport, MA: Element, 1994.

*Asa Hershoff, D.C., N.D., *Homeopathic Medicines for Musculoskeletal Healing*. Berkeley: North Atlantic, 1997.

Colin Lessell, M.D., D.D.S., *The World Traveller's Manual of Homoeopathy*. Saffron, Walden, England: C.W. Daniel, 1993.

*Andrew Lockie, M.D., and Nicola Geddes, M.D., *The Women's Guide to Homeopathy*. New York: St. Martin's, 1994.

*Richard Moskowitz, M.D., *Homeopathic Medicine for Pregnancy and Childbirth*. Berkeley: North Atlantic, 1992.

*Michael A. Schmidt, *Healing Childhood Ear Infections: Prevention, Home Care, and Alternative Treatments*. Berkeley: North Atlantic, 1996.

*Steven Subotnick, D.P.M., D.C., *Sports and Exercise Injuries: Conventional, Homeopathic, and Alternative Treatments*. Berkeley: North Atlantic, 1991.

*Dana Ullman, M.P.H., *Homeopathic Medicine for Children and Infants*. New York: Jeremy Tarcher/Putnam, 1992.

homeopathy a–z

*Robert Ullman, N.D., and Judyth Reichenberg-Ullman, N.D., M.S.W., *Ritalin-Free Kids: Homeopathic Treatment of ADD and other Behavioral and Learning Problems*. Rocklin, CA: Prima, 1996.

*Janet Zand, N.D., Rachel Walton, R.N., and Bob Rountree, M.D., *Smart Medicine for a Healthier Child*. New York: Avery, 1994.

Philosophy and Methodology

Note: Books on homeopathic philosophy and methodology are primarily for students or practitioners of homeopathy, although anyone with a serious interest in the healing process will learn much from them.

*Samuel Hahnemann, M.D., *Organon of Medicine*. New Delhi, India. Reprint. A newly translated edition which is considered the most accurate is: *The Organon of the Medical Art*, Seattle: Birdcage, 1996.

*James Tyler Kent, M.D., *Lectures on Homoeopathic Philosophy*. Berkeley: North Atlantic, 1979. Reprint.

Gerhard Koehler, M.D., *The Handbook of Homeopathy*. Rochester, VT.: Healing Arts, 1987.

H.A. Roberts, M.D., *The Principles and Art of Cure by Homoeopathy*. New Delhi: B. Jain. Reprint.

*Todd Rowe, M.D., *Homeopathic Methodology*. Berkeley: North Atlantic, 1998.

*Rajan Sankaran, *The Spirit of Homeopathy*. Bombay: Homeopathic Medical Publishers, 1991.

*George Vithoulkas, *The Science of Homeopathy*. New York: Grove, 1980.

*Elizabeth Hubbard Wright, M.D., *A Brief Study Course in Homeopathy*. St. Louis: Formur, 1977.

SOURCE OF HOMEOPATHIC BOOKS, TAPES, AND SOFTWARE

Homeopathic Educational Services
2124 Kittredge St.
Berkeley, CA 94704 ▪ (510) 649-0294
Website: www.homeopathic.com
E-mail: mail@homeopathic.com

** Most of the sources of homeopathic medicines (listed previously) are also sources of books on homeopathy, although they do not have an extensive selection.